PUBLIC ART

GARRISON ROOTS

designing the world's best PUBLIC ART

First published in Australia in 2002 by
The Images Publishing Group Pty Ltd
ABN 89 059 734 431
6 Bastow Place, Mulgrave, Victoria, 3170, Australia
Telephone: +613 9561 5544 Facsimile: +613 9561 4860
Email: books@images.com.au
Website: www.imagespublishinggroup.com

Copyright © The Images Publishing Group Pty Ltd
The Images Publishing Group Reference Number: 487

National Library of Australia
Cataloguing-in-Publication data

Roots, Garrison.
Designing the world's best public art.

Includes index.
ISBN: 1 86470 082 3

1. Public art – United States. I. Title

709.73

Designed by The Graphic Image Studio Pty Ltd, Mulgrave, Australia
Film by Mission Productions Ltd., Hong Kong
Printed in Hong Kong by the Paramount Printing Company Limited

IMAGES has included on its website a page for special notices in relation to this and our
other publications. It includes updates in relation to the information printed in our books.
Please visit this site: www.imagespublishinggroup.com

13   INTRODUCTION

CONTENTS

ARTISTS

18   **TERRY ALLEN**
Notre Denver, 1994   19
Modern Communication, 1995   20
Corporate Head, 1990   21
Belief, 1999   23

24   **JOAN LLAVERIA ARASA**
Line 3 of Valencia's Subway, 1999   25
Sculptural Garden of Font del riu, 1999   27
Cultural Center, "La Asuncion", 1998   29
Gran Caribe Hotel, 1998   30

32   **ED CARPENTER**
Market Street Pedestrian Bridge, 2001   33
Flying Bridge, 1998   35
Hokkaido Sports Center, 1999   36
Sphere, 1997   39
Broadway Pumphouse Sculpture, 2000   41

42   **BRAD GOLDBERG**
Continuum, 2000   43
Bloomington Waters, 1996   45
Prince of Peace Catholic Community, 1994   46
Pegasus Plaza, 1994   48
Mears Park, 1993   47

50   **DOUGLAS HOLLIS**
A Sound Garden, 1983   51
Water Songs, 1996   52
Oionos, 1997   53
Mountain Mirage, 1999   54
Tidal Park, 1988   56
Weather Pavilion, 1993   57

CONTENTS continued

58   KRISTIN JONES AND ANDREW GINZEL

Metronome, 1999   59

Oculus, 1999   60

Sounding, 1994   62

Parenthesis, 1998   63

Mnemonics, 1992   65

66   STACY LEVY

Seeing the Path of the Wind, 1991   67

Watercourse, 1996   69

What's in the Wind, 1991   70

Medal of Honor Memorial for Pennsylvania Recipients, 1997   71

72   WINIFRED LUTZ

Correspondence/Congruence (Paradigm), 1995   73

Site Unseen/Fluid Bodies, 1998   74

The Garden, 1992-1997   75

Reclamation Garden, 1996   76

$\frac{\text{Threshold/Interface/Transition}}{\text{When}}$, 1997   77

78   WILLIAM MAXWELL

Echo, 1999   79

Endangered, 1994   80

Pandora, 1989   81

82   ANNA VALENTINA MURCH

Skydance, 1995   83

Cycles, 1997   85

Skytones, 1998   87

Light Passageway, 1993   89

Memorial Union North Courtyard, 1993   90

92   **JODY PINTO**

Boone Sculpture Garden, 1995–2000   93

Beacon Overlook and Restrooms, 1995–2001   94

Lantern Bridge, 1995–2001   95

Light Islands, 1999   97

98   **ANTONETTE ROSATO**

The Pattern that Connects, 1995   99

Immigrant Desire/American Longing: The Vestibule, 1998   100

Immigrant Desire/American Longing: The Return, 1998   101

Middle Knowledge, 1999   103

Kinetic Light/Air Curtain, 1994   104

106   **DEAN RUCK**

Big Bubble, 1998   107

O House, 1995   108

Tree House, 2000   109

Jewel, 2000   111

112   **NORIE SATO**

Dallas Convention Center Expansion Project, 1993   113

Biochemistry Waltz, 1998   115

Brief Cases, 1998   116

Gallivan Plaza Light Rail Station, 2000   119

Courthouse Station, 2000   117

CONTENTS continued

PUBLIC ART PROGRAMS

122 BROWARD COUNTY CULTURAL AFFAIRS COUNCIL

Accordant Zones, 1994/Barbara Neijna and Ned Smyth — 123
Calypso, 1998/Tobey Archer — 124
Everglades Tresspass, 2000/Carl Cheng — 126
Light Cylinders, 1996–2001/Jody Pinto — 127

128 CITY OF SAN DIEGO COMMISSION FOR ART AND CULTURE

Metro Biosolids Center, 1998/Richard Turner — 129
The Alvarado Garden, 1998/Robert Millar — 130
Great Balboa Park Landfill Exposition, 1997/Cindy Zimmerman — 133

134 CULTURAL ARTS COUNCIL OF HOUSTON

Countree Music, 1999/Terry Allen — 135
Seven Wonders, 1998/Mel Chin — 136
Elevator Core, 2000/Rachel Hecker — 138
Metro Bus Shelter, 1999/Rachel Hecker, Benito Huerta and Richard Turner — 139

142 MTA METRO ART

Vermont/Santa Monica Station, 1999/Robert Millar — 145
People Coming/People Going, 1996/Richard Wyatt — 146
Crenshaw Stories, 1995/Buzz Spector — 149
I Dreamed I Could Fly, 1993/Jonathan Borofsky — 143

150 MIAMI-DADE ART IN PUBLIC PLACES

A Walk on the Beach, Phase I, 1995, Phase II, 1999/Michele Oka Doner — 151
36th Street Wall, 1996/Martha Schwartz — 153
Harmonic Runway, 1995/Christopher Janney — 154
Aqua/Botanica, 1997/Ed Carpenter, Mike McCulloch and John Rogers — 157

158   **PHOENIX ARTS COMMISSION**

Papago Park/City Boundary, 1992/Jody Pinto   159

An Open Book, 1996/Mayme Kratz, Debra L. Hopkins, Valerie Badala Homer   161

Paradise Lane Bridge,1998/Linnea Glatt with HDR Engineering   162

The Grasshopper Bridge 1997/Ed Carpenter   162

Nisbet Road Pedestrian Bridge,1998/Laurie Lundquist in partnership with HDR
Engineering   163

164   **SAN FRANCISCO ARTS COMMISSION**

Functional and Fantasy Stair/Cyclone Fragment, 1996/Alice Aycock   165

Constellation, 1996/Nayland Blake   166

Jury Assembly Room, 1997-98/Lewis Desoto   167

Civic Center Courthouse Entry Doors, Security Gates, and Door Handles,
1997–1998/Albert Paley   167

Untitled, 1996/Ann Hamilton and Ann Chamberlain   168

170   **SAN JOSE PUBLIC ART PROGRAM**

Origin, 1999/Brad Goldberg, Beliz Brother and Joseph McShane   171

Untitled, 1999/Ann Chamberlain and Victor Mario Zaballa   173

Jump Cuts, 1996/Elizabeth Diller and Ricardo Scofidio, with Paul Lewis   176

182   **GENERAL CREDITS**

188   **PHOTOGRAPHY CREDITS**

191   **INDEX**

192   **ACKNOWLEDGMENTS**

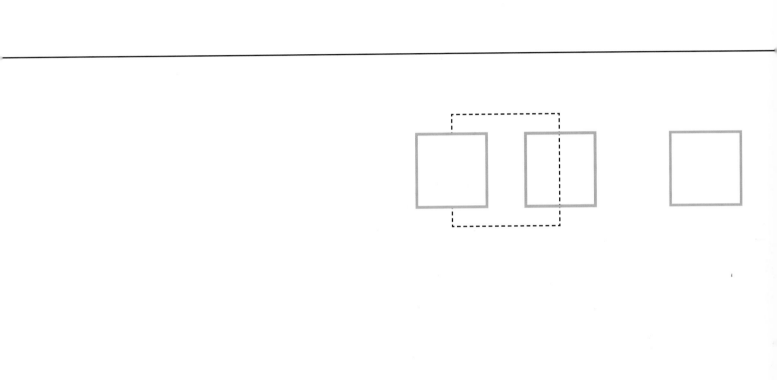

INTRODUCTION

A wealth of public art exists, particularly in the United States, which has followed the processes necessary for the creation of art for the public, from the public. The development of public art follows a process unprecedented in the production of any other art. It is the meeting of minds on many levels. It is visible and obvious, and open to the criticism of anyone who experiences its outward presentation. However, what is seen of public art is usually only the tip of the collaboration between artist, community groups, civic planners, and architects. An original idea is scrutinised from the outset, sometimes diluted or expanded from a specific focus, and presented as a response to a variety of factors. ● As I sit at my desk my thoughts are strangely condensed about this book. I know it does not address all the issues I have named above, but I am not sure it could, given the format and the particular group of artists who have responded to my queries. In front of me is a picture of myself surrounded by two lovely ladies, all of us sitting atop the stoop of an Airstream trailer where I lived as a child. We have just survived my first birthday. It will be many years before I have any concept about art, and much less public art. However, I suppose that the Airstream was my first experience of American public art. After all, it accomplishes in a practical way, just about everything I have heard anyone want from a public artwork. It is visually stunning, an American icon, historically based, made of a durable material, requires little maintenance, is somewhat inexpensive, and does not offend the political, religious or moral sensibilities of too many people. ● This book features some of the finest works of public art ever presented in one volume. Each artist and each program is considered to be among the world's best. Public artists enter into consultation with a community, learn about its mindset and generate thought-provoking works and

INTRODUCTION continued

installations in some very public settings. Each artist has been commissioned to present their art in civic and transit spaces, in retail and corporate areas, and in galleries. ● Public art should be about inclusion, tolerance, friendship, community, the environment, ritual, and an appreciation of other cultures in the global village. It must challenge and be subversive for all the right reasons, rather than conform to a package that does not disturb the prevailing physical or emotional state. Artists should act as the conscience of the culture. The role of the public artist has evolved, but continues to be underscored by a need to communicate the experience of a particular community. ● However, if one bases theory about art on the idea that it is derived from an emotional state tempered by the viewer's experience, then perhaps much of what is offered as public art has little to do with public art. Public art is often directed by the wishes of the client who commissions the work, thereby diluting the expression of the community in everyday existence. In this way, the artist works within a profession as a means of subsistence, thus limiting the creation of true art. As an example, some public art concepts have to do with history, multiculturalism, and a sense of place, as they relate to a particular project. Although they are good concepts, they seldom lead to a strong emotional interpretation by a particular artist because of demands by the client to improve their understanding of the community and how they want it to be represented. ● Public art is subject to an aesthetic scrutiny which is unsurpassed in modern cultural history. The artist must gain the support of committees comprising members that range from interested civic-minded individuals to construction project leaders, many of whom have little or no knowledge of art. Those who may have a solid background in the arts, such as program directors, architects, and designers, are sadly outnumbered and their vision often ambushed. Therefore, the democratic process breaks down, ultimately destroying the possibility of producing art in a public place, for the public, that challenges the public. This is also based on the general confusion that art and design are one and the same. Although both are of equal importance regarding cultural development, and indeed share many of the same attributes, they are in many ways distinctively different. ● I find it interesting, that in spite of the inherent politics of any public process, healthy art is produced. It achieves and offers a strong, challenging, sensitive, and intelligent aesthetic for public consumption. Good work is designed and created despite limitations being placed on it from its inception. To the critically disposed, it can be seen as the difference between a technically mastered 'picture' and art that happens to be in the form of a 'picture'. This debate is ongoing. ● This book showcases the artists whose efforts and disposition were able to rise above the often confused debates to produce work that firmly deserves to be called art in public places. The struggle to be inclusive and the emotional ideals behind each work of art is timeless. It seems increasingly difficult to offer art for public consumption for fear of someone finding it offensive. We need respectful dialog to find answers. Artists for the public are bound to act as the conscience of the culture. After all, without great public art and architecture the ever-growing onslaught of tableau architecture as represented in fast food restaurants, amusement parks, shopping malls and car washes will continue tearing at our aesthetic sensibilities.

Garrison Roots

Professor of Fine Arts, Area Coordinator of Sculpture,
University of Colorado, Boulder, Colorado, USA

ALLEN

CARPENTER

HOLLIS

LEVY

ARASA

GOLDBERG

JONES/GINZEL

LUTZ

MAXWELL

PINTO

MURCH

ROSATO

RUCK

SATO

ARTISTS

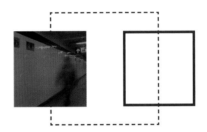 

Notre Denver, 1994

Modern Communication, 1995

Corporate Head, 1990

Belief, 1999

TERRY ALLEN

Terry Allen's viewers might often be caught looking back, wondering if they really saw what they just saw, then turning back around and laughing to themselves. Who is he kidding, but all of us? His sarcastic surrealism catches our attention by poking an elbow into the ribs of any given state of contemporary societal mess. The artist preferred not to provide an official artist statement, so we have allowed him instead to elucidate the following projects in his own words. We trust you'll get the picture.

Notre Denver, 1994

The baggage claim areas of a busy airport have been adorned with bronze gargoyles. A bird-beaked gargoyle overlooks the domestic baggage claim area and a Notre Dame-faced gargoyle overlooks the international area. Each squats inside an elevated bronze suitcase and look down as protectors of luggage. They are scaled to the size of a twelve-year-old boy, and the suitcases have been molded from a real Samsonite suitcase. Rumours abound that any problems that were being experienced with the airport baggage systems ceased with the installation of the gargoyles.

Modern Communication, 1995

A life-sized bronze businessman stands on a briefcase with his tie wrapped around his eyes, his fingers in his ears, and a shoe in his mouth. The figure is located in a small square and faces out from the communication center, and across the street toward city hall. The city court building is directly to the right and the jail is to his left. The majority of viewers who confront him each day are police officers, law breakers, lawyers, and judges, some firemen, and a general assortment of city employees.

CORPORATE HEAD, 1990

A slightly, larger-than-life bronze businessman bends over with his head stuck in the side of a building. A poem by Philip Levine, also titled *Corporate Head*, has been engraved onto a plaque into the sidewalk, directly behind the heels of his nice shoes.

They said

I had a head

For business.

They said to get ahead

I had to lose my head.

They said

Be concrete

& I became

concrete.

They said,

Go, my son,

multiply,

divide, conquer.

I did my best.

In order to read this poem, the reader must assume approximately the same position as the statue.

BELIEF, 1999

A large bronze leaf (20x20 feet with a 20-foot stem) has been placed lying on the ground at the steps of a world-leading cancer research center designed by Frank O. Gehry. The work is intended for people to interact with, lie, and eat. It has been entitled BELIEF because it seemed to make sense with the human endeavor taking place inside the building.

Line 3 of Valencia's Subway

Sculptural Garden of 'Font del riu'

Cultural Center, 'La Asuncion'

Gran Caribe Hotel

JOAN LLAVERIA I ARASA

Llavería explains that he is influenced by specific concepts and focuses, rather than by other artists or movements. He works on a system of project development, using a combination of experimental approaches from both the beginning of the 20th century and traditional methods, to transform ideas into substance. ● Materials are combined with an objective and a strategy to generate a process for each work—each work is then related to the space in which it is located. Outdoor locations usually feature stone and metal, and blend with the natural environment or nearby structures. At other times, meaningful microcosms are brought into play with the inclusion of vegetation or water. ● The starting point for each work is usually an historical focus. It stimulates and orientates both interest and motivation for each project. In the same way, the environment has an identity which is greater than the natural surroundings, or as the context in which the work is located. It is the cultural ambience which is a fundamental principle sustaining each work. ● Llavería describes his work as part of a process that involves an intent to establish a dialogue with the cultural significance of the location and its point in time. The result is the geometric formulation of shapes, and the expressive combination of materials. ● This artist's work is a search for harmony through an affinity or a contrast with natural forms, and the completion, if this is the case, of architectural forms. His work is not based on a closed series of personal concepts, but rather on the constant intention to provide the conditions to generate an open dialog with the resonances, facts, and events that may be found in the location in which each work will take shape.

LINE 3 OF VALENCIA'S SUBWAY

This work in a railway subway gives the impression of a place of shelter, a strategic subterranean place used during military conflict. It was employed as a refuge during the bombing of London in the Second World War. The work is more than a rhetoric recourse to connect with an event of historic circumstance. It is a potent sign that makes the station's space unique by endowing it with an expressive character.

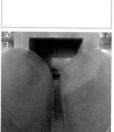

SCULPTURAL GARDEN OF 'FONT DEL RIU'

Modernisation has caused the loss of many customs associated with traditional Mediterranean lifestyle, a freedom of time that allowed conversation, dialog, and contemplation. Similarly, some trees that once had enormous importance have declined in productive interest. Nevertheless, their forms are usually full of meaning and cultural significance. This is true of the Ceratonia Silicua which is a leguminous tree of unique characteristics and with clear Mediterranean ties. The work, in this case, intends to underline the presence of this tree, and also, create a space at its base for deliberate recreation of time by employing a small fountain. An ambience for contemplation and tranquillity is created through the soft murmur of the water.

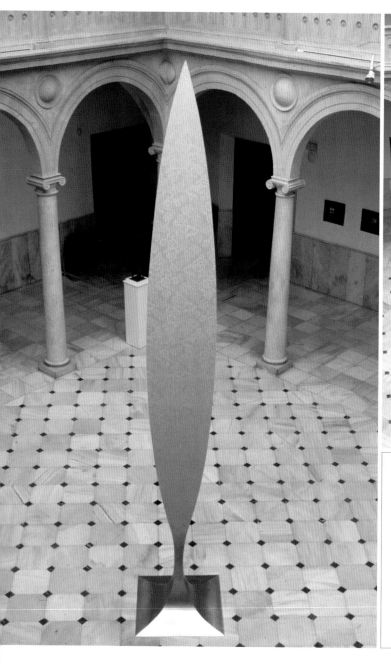

Cultural Center, 'La Asuncion'

With the passing of time and successive remodeling, the cloister, which dates from the Renaissance, lost its original character of secluded devotion, and had no specific use. The project includes a work which evokes the form of a Cyprus tree, which is both symbolic and reminiscent of the spiritual elevation and devotion that originally presided at this place.

Gran Caribe Hotel

Omeros, a book of poetry written by Derek Walcott, tells of the epic adventure of the search for liberty. The artwork was found in the Isla de la Juventud (The Isle of Youth) in Cuba, and now stands upon a seaside hillock. It has the form of a small temple in dialogue with the sea, and is used as a metaphor for space without boundaries, and the desire to find Utopia.

Market Street Pedestrian Bridge, 2001

Flying Bridge, 1998

Hokkaido Sports Center, 1999

Sphere, 1997

Broadway Pumphouse Sculpture, 2000

ED CARPENTER

Ed Carpenter is an artist specializing in large-scale public installations ranging from architectural sculpture to infrastructure design. Since 1973 he has completed scores of projects for public, corporate, and ecclesiastical clients. Working internationally from his studio in Portland, Oregon, Carpenter collaborates personally with a variety of expert consultants, subcontractors, and studio assistants. He personally oversees every step of each commission, and installs them himself with a crew of longtime helpers, except in the case of the largest objects, such as bridges. ● While an interest in light has been virtually fundamental in all of Carpenter's work, he also embraces commissions which require new approaches and skills. This openness has led to an increasing variety in his commissions, and a wide range of sites, and materials. His recent projects include bridges, towers, gateways, and roof-top structures, as well as interior sculptures, windows, and skylights. In each case an ambivalent relationship with the surroundings is sought, simultaneously integrating and intervening the organic and technological, and the sentient and engineered. He is known as an eager and open-minded collaborator as well as technical innovator. His use of cold bent tempered glass elements, programmed artificial lighting, and unusual tension structures have broken new ground in architectural art. ● Carpenter is the grandson of a painter/sculptor, and the stepson of an architect in whose office he worked summers as a teenager. He studied architectural glass art under artists in England and Germany during the early 1970s, and now lives with his wife and two children in the Coast Range Mountains west of Portland.

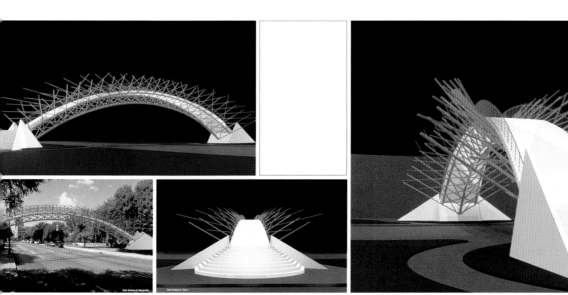

Market Street Pedestrian Bridge, 2001

Here the artist uses the imagery of local desert flora, while incorporating themes of light and color interwoven throughout the convention center architecture. The bridge uses an expressive painted steel truss to recall rays of light, sprays of water, and exotic southwestern plant life. It is a unique and exuberant expression of the spirit of San Antonio.

Flying Bridge, 1998

Hovering beneath the atrium's 88-foot high skylight, Flying Bridge spans metaphorically and physically between the biology and chemistry departments in Central Washington University's Dean Science Building. The aluminum structure and dicroic glass panels play in the light, casting moving shadows and projections when the sun is aligned. At night, special lighting casts colored light onto architectural surfaces.

Hokkaido Sports Center, 1999

Carpenter's objective was to create a delicate and transparent tracery of cables and glass strips. In the daylight, the cone of glass strips and stainless steel cables reflect and project subtly changing colors in kinetic patterns. At night the entire pavilion is a glowing lantern which sparkles with delicate luminosity. The structure is so airy and transparent that from some angles it seems to disappear.

SPHERE, 1997

Lending focus to the center of the school's kinesis, SPHERE consists of an enigmatic glowing sphere, suspended above the grand stair and connected by cables, in suggestion of the interconnectedness and collaborative spirit of the Carlson school. Cold bent tempered plate and dichroic glass continuously illuminate it day and night, cyclically changing coloration, simultaneously projecting images on the walls of the atrium.

Broadway Pumphouse Sculpture, 2000

Carpenter has designed a gateway sculpture which uses the pumphouse as a pedestal to achieve monumental stature. Travelers entering the city will see it silhouetted against the skyline. Its imagery celebrates the transportation and manufacturing industries which have occupied that part of the city over the years and will serve as a reminder of the hard working, gritty character of this vital neighborhood.

Continuum, 2000

Bloomington Waters, 1996

Prince of Peace Catholic Community, 1994

Mears Park, 1994

Pegasus Plaza, 1994

BRAD GOLDBERG

Brad Goldberg is an artist who sees his work as a fusion between sculpture, the landscape, and the built environment. Sculptures are seen not as isolated objects, but rather as spirit-creating components of larger spatial experiences. The desire to work with the environment as a whole has necessitated expanding outside the traditional role of a studio sculptor, into an area which might be termed landscape sculpture. Ultimately, each new project generates a unique, spontaneous response encompassing the total aspect of a specific place or circumstance, often entailing many of the complexities of working on large environmental projects. Brad works as an idea generator, and this has lead to collaborative efforts with other artists, architects, design professionals, civic leaders, and communities. These efforts have resulted in many projects on which, in addition to his private work, Brad has worked conceptually in the creation of site-specific sculptures, parks, gardens, interior spaces, furniture, and landscape installation. Brad resides in Dallas where he keeps his studio. He frequently travels internationally to work on projects and to maintain a world perspective. 'In time,' he states, 'with many experiences layered over one another, I am hoping my work will reflect a cultural collage, more in keeping with artistic truths than passing fashions'.

Continuum, 2000

Continuum is an entire city block of streetscape which was designed by the artist. It includes black granite boulders cut to metamorphose into smoothly polished cubes, which have been laid in a circular space. This space continues into the lobby to create a seamless continuum between the indoor and outdoor environments. The stones are sited on a pixilated 'carpet' of black and white exterior granite paving and interior terrazzo flooring. Three white, carved granite vertical monoliths flank the entrance. A series of solid black granite planters serve as seating and contain gingko, serviceberry trees, and annual plantings.

BLOOMINGTON WATERS, 1996

The intention was to create art with a judicious use of water. The vessel or cistern symbolizes the precious nature of water and creates a shallow stream that meanders through the plaza. The richly carved surface captures light, shadow, and water like organic lines. Water, its precious environmental quality, and the need for better public education are thoughts that seeded this idea.

PRINCE OF PEACE CATHOLIC COMMUNITY, 1994

The central platform of the sanctuary was conceived as an abstraction of a natural yet ritualistic landform. It provides a 360-degree centering experience focused on the liturgical actions of the church. A focus upon the platform is created, in which people are comfortable, seated together in view of one another, and involved as participants and not as spectators.

Mears Park, 1994

The overall design of the park refers to the geological as well as the human history of the area. It engenders a dialogue between the area's natural beauty and the built environment. The park concept contains a vision of a future in which people are stewards of nature and the spaces they inhabit, which in return are vessels for their activities and enjoyment.

Pegasus Plaza, 1994

Conceived to bring forth a sense of life and creative spirit to revitalize downtown, PEGASUS PLAZA incorporates many layers of history and culture to create a strong sense of Dallas. The place is imbued with personal meaning, universal inclusiveness, and a sense of belonging which enriches the lives of its users. The Pegasus myth and Dallas are strong symbols of life rising out of death.

A Sound Garden, 1983

Water Songs, 1996

Oionos, 1997

Mountain Mirage, 1999

Tidal Park, 1988 with artist Charles Fahlan

Weather Pavilion, 1993

DOUGLAS HOLLIS

Douglas Hollis was born in Ann Arbor, Michigan in 1948, and continued to live there throughout the years of his college education. From an early age he had a deep interest in Native American culture. He began to meet Indian people, first in Michigan and the Mid-West, and later began travelling in Oklahoma to live for periods of time with Indian families. He received a unique worldview from these people which has strongly influenced his life. ● In the early 1970s he searched for new ways to talk about landscape and the forces which are consistently affecting it. The artist's first excursion into public art occurred in 1977. Hollis has developed his work in sound structures and landscape, working on-site and establishing rapport with the dynamics of the site and with the people who encounter these places. ● The early 1980s were a pivotal period for Hollis, primarily because of the major permanent commission of A SOUND GARDEN for the NOAA in Seattle, Washington. It was during the development of these more orchestrated works that he began to realize the necessity to perceive the long-range implications of these places. Hollis thus challenged himself to create 'good vessels'; frameworks, which people would want to inhabit and which would age well and increase in meaning as time flowed over them. ● Throughout the 1990s Hollis has gone on to complete many large-scale projects, often collaborating with other artists, architects, and landscape architects, and making places which have an oasis-like quality, where people can pause to catch their spiritual breath in the midst of their everyday lives.

A SOUND GARDEN, 1983

A SOUND GARDEN is located on a wave of land overlooking Lake Washington in Seattle. It is a poetic forest of linear 21-foot-high steel towers that support wind-activated organ pipes mounted on vanes that move to face the wind. As people wander along the 300-foot custom brick and gravel path or sit on perforated steel benches, they encounter a zenith of shoreline, light, wind, and sound as portrayed through the organ pipes.

WATER SONGS, 1996

WATER SONGS is a series of connected water elements and seating along the entry to a library and hydrology laboratory. The elements include the source pool, riverbed, a canal seatwall, and a perpetual vortex. The work explores the subtle sonic and visual aspects of water, as well as climate modification through evaporative cooling. The work also includes a semi-circular seating area in the shade of an oak tree that can be used for talks or casual sitting.

Oionos, 1997

A wind-activated 28-foot-long stainless-steel 'quill' appears to write in the air while the sun projects, through a cut-out panel, a quotation from Shakespeare's 'The Tempest' on the plaza paving. The work celebrates the tools humans have invented to convey knowledge over time and space.

MOUNTAIN MIRAGE, 1999

A 30x60 foot free-form pool frames an array of 3,232 vertical water jets that
create a three-dimensional model of the Front Range of the Rocky
Mountains. The work adds a refreshing combination of humidity, sound,
and negative ions to the Great Hall space of the terminal at the Denver
International Airport. It also adds a contemplative kinetic visual focal point
to greet people as they arrive.

Tidal Park, 1988 with artist Charles Fahlan

The spiral form of the 'Tide Clock' element fills and empties during a 12-foot tidal cycle, creating a man-made tide pool and marine observatory. The 'Wave Gazing Gallery' is a place to look out at Puget Sound and listen to the waves breaking underneath. There is an aeolian harp at the top of the gallery, surrounding an opening in the roof that frames the sky. A similar opening to the deck below allows a view of the waves.

Weather Pavilion, 1993

This stainless-steel structure is located in the corner of a school playground looking out at the East River and mid-town Manhattan. It is an observatory where the students and faculty can investigate weather phenomena, geographic location, and geology. Traditional weather instruments are housed in the pavilion columns. A wind organ pipe forms a kinetic spire at the top of the dome overlooking the 'geo-puzzle' bench. Each is designed to help link science, art, music, and myth.

Metronome, 1999

Oculus, 1999

Sounding, 1994

Parenthesis, 1998

Mnemonics, 1992

KRISTIN JONES and ANDREW GINZEL

The intrinsic nature of Jones and Ginzel's work is collaborative. Jones and Ginzel say that the impossibility of knowing either time or truth, present or past, is at the core of their fascination with the world and has been the genesis for their work for more than sixteen years. Their thinking begins with the context and situation, and weaves into question the basics which may be right in front of us, yet which we usually cannot see. 'Ultimately, we are interested in the impossible brevity of life. Through our work we have sought to challenge a heightened awareness of mortality…of time.' ● The artists are driven by a wilful desire to question, to cause reflection on a place, and a time of place, in which the viewer is directly addressed. Engaging in the essential questions asked by the work, the viewer becomes part of the collaborative process, and transforms the perception of their very existence. ● The works are rigorous experiments that take place in a wide range of situations, public, private spaces, and a stage where the artists attempt to reveal things that are universal and fundamental to all. They aspire to create work that is almost as transparent as artwork, while being very much present physically, and very much part of a given place as well. ● Their work is an outcry against cultural homogenization, against the emptiness and banality caused by the economy of construction, and by mass production. It is an attempt to focus on and to intensify the experience of living. ● 'Our dream for the future is to seek opportunities that we ourselves initiate, choosing empty places that engage the banal void, so as to explore realms that address an even wider audience, beyond a privileged realm specific to a particular culture. Working within the vocabulary of a chosen situation, we hope to transform the commonplace into what can awaken and astonish.'

Metronome, 1999

Conceived to confront the person on the street, the work suggests an instant and infinity, the astronomical sequence and the geological epoch relative to the place itself, and to the individual's heartbeat and breath. The work is an attempt to question our place in time by creating metaphorical bridges that span the scale of time, simultaneously implying the impossibility of knowing time.

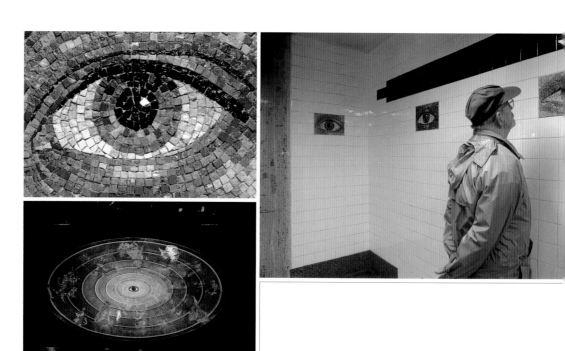

Oculus, 1999

Oculus is a constellation of mosaics in an underground
labyrinth in a large subway station in lower Manhattan.
A magnificent stone and glass eye at the center of an
ultramarine vortex floor focuses hundreds of distinct
individual eyes throughout the station. The detailed
renderings of the eye, the most telling, fragile, and
vulnerable human feature, offers a profound sense
of intimacy within a raw, cold, and empty place,
creating dialogue between the infrastructure and
those who use it.

Sounding, 1994

Sounding is an investigative layering of fluctuating events and perceptions. A person entering finds an illuminated cobalt blue glass archway of tunnel, from where a wave of light originates. A line of individual cobalt blue light passes, and the archway dissolves. A 'shadow' of the Liberty Bell sounds from a hidden source. The blue archway re-ignites, and a blue 'constellation' of lights are simultaneously extinguished.

Parenthesis, 1998

Two spirals, one forming the terrazzo floor, the other suspended overhead, create a double cone focused on the brass image of Wisconsin at the center point of the floor. A mirror set into the central cone catches one reflection, grasping a moment of one life. The Enigma, a large levitated boulder with a dark interior void, suggests everything which is outside our capacity for understanding.

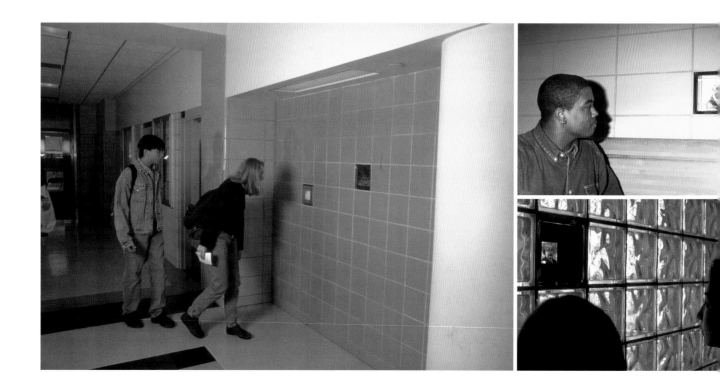

Mnemonics, 1992

Four hundred random glass enclosures mortared into masonry walls exist throughout the building. Some refer to one year of Stuyvesant history, and others are to be filled by future generations of Stuyvesant graduates. Fragments of the Mayan pyramids, ashes from Hjerculaneum, water from the Nile and Ganges Rivers, leaves from the sacred Bo tree, a fragment of the Great Wall of China—each relic composes a vast visual library of clues for an extended period of time.

Seeing the Path of the Wind, 1991

Watercourse, 1996

What's in the Wind, 1991

Medal of Honor Memorial for
Pennsylvania Recipients, 1997

STACY LEVY

Levy has an interest in both art and science. She works within the two fields, using art as a vehicle for translating the patterns and processes of the natural world into the language of human understanding. ● The art of Levy focuses on a premise that from the 20th century science has been employed to translate nature, but from a disadvantage because it has a limited vocabulary to understand the world. 'The language of science is one of separation rather than integration, and scientific discourse has eliminated subjective experience in favor of objective data.' ● Levy believes that art has a freer tongue and many languages at its disposal. 'Since art has no debt to empirical positivism, it is able to bind the separate views of science and culture to formulate another way of picturing the earth.' ● By describing occurrences which seem commonplace, like rain or tidal movement, or phenomena which are unseen such as the path of the wind, or the microscopic forms of life in sea or river water, Levy's art brings the overlooked forces of nature into view. ● Her installations and public works investigate aspects of the natural processes which make each site identifiable. Wind is brought indoors to blow across a compass of 1,000 flags, a river is mapped with the waters from its tributaries, and a season of rainfall is collected. Each work serves as sculptural interventions which make the invisible forces of nature more salient to the viewer. ● Levy explains that she attempts to look again at the scientific explanation of natural systems by redefining their visual components. By emeshing the clarity of diagrams and the accessibility of maps with the more visceral sense of the site, Levy creates an instant of wonder and understanding for the viewer.

Seeing the Path of the Wind, 1991

A weather station placed on the seventh floor balcony of the gallery sends wind speed and direction data to a weather station inside the gallery. The station turns off and on eight fans at the cardinal point of a 30-foot diameter compass made from 1,000 flags. As the wind direction outdoors changes, the corresponding fans turn on to stimulate the wind blowing through the building. Depending on the velocity of the wind, the flags would ripple or fully extend.

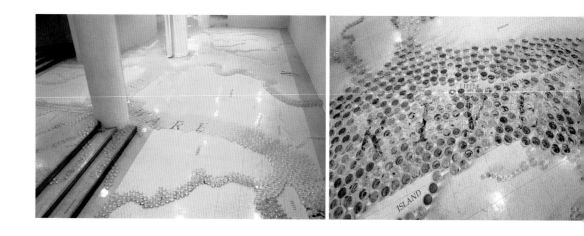

WATERCOURSE, 1996

Over 8,000 cups map the Delaware River and its tributaries. The width and depth of each stream, creek, and river are represented by the different height and width of the cups. The cups are filled with water collected from the area which each represents. Historic creeks dating from the 1700s, now 'culverted' or filled, are represented by overturned cups. As the exhibition progresses, the water evaporates and is replenished. Various forms of algae grow in the different creeks and rivers depending on the composition of the water.

WHAT'S IN THE WIND, 1991

WHAT'S IN THE WIND explores how the air around us is affected by many sources, like the smoke from distant factories, to the exhaust from cars which have just parked. The translucent blue windsocks indicate the direction of the wind over stone dials set in the lawn. These stone dials let the viewer read where the wind is coming from and what it brings, in terms of weather, air pollution, and suspended particles.

Medal of Honor Memorial for Pennsylvania Recipients, 1997

Thirteen radiating arcs, representing the conflicts and wars in which Pennsylvanians received the Medal of Honor, symbolize the tides of war. Granite stones set into the arcs identify the medal recipients with the date and location of their deeds. At the far end of the memorial lie the shores of peace; a grove of 13 trees and rough-faced seating stones inscribed with the word 'Remember'.

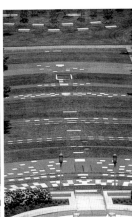

Correspondence/Congruence (Paradigm), 1995

Site Unseen/Fluid Bodies, 1998

The Garden, 1992–1997

Reclamation Garden, 1996

Threshold/Interface/Transition
When , 1997

WINIFRED LUTZ

The site-integrated sculptural installations of Winifred Lutz are known for their 'remarkable sensitivity to the site, and the creation of works that underscore the vegetative and social processes that determine the discrete history of a place'. Since 1975 she has built major installations and public projects in the United States and Europe. All the works seek to acknowledge the confluence of factors unique to a location—they engage the interplay of the built and natural environments, and the phenomena of available light and changing seasons. She is interested in uncovering the urban and natural history of a site to reveal the implicit layers and boundaries of physical memory, which qualify its identity as a place for the surrounding community. In her outdoor works, stone, plant communities, water, paths, and architectural elements are used to intensify the solitary, contemplative, and on-the-ground experience of a site. The artist feels that each place should embody the complexity and transience of the natural world, while reminding the visitor of the interdependence of abstraction and physical experience that is the basis of understanding anything. ● Winifred Lutz is also well known for her expertise and art in making handmade paper. She has lectured nationally and internationally and published papers on the unique casting and other techniques she has developed for the medium. This work has been exhibited in Europe, Asia, North and South America, and Israel. ● Currently a Laura Carnell Professor, teaching sculpture at Tyler School of Art, Temple University, Philadelphia, Pennsylvania, she lives and works in Huntington Valley, Pennsylvania. She has been the recipient of many awards, including a US National Endowment for the Arts Fellowship, and a PEW Fellowship in the Arts. Her work is represented in both museum and private collections across the United States.

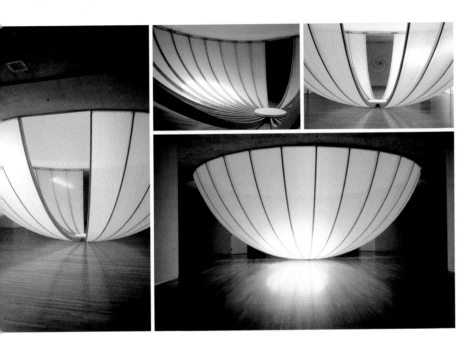

CORRESPONDENCE/CONGRUENCE (PARADIGM), 1995

CORRESPONDENCE/CONGRUENCE (PARADIGM) is a 30-foot-diameter inverted dome placed directly below the center's domed skylight. On either end of the two entrances through the inverted dome are large eight-foot-diameter wall drawings. At the center is a cast white concrete basin.

Site Unseen/Fluid Bodies, 1998

Site Unseen/Fluid Bodies is based on ten ponds on campus at the College of DuPaige. Across the wall are nine of the ponds, each placed with its north-south axis vertical, north on top. The tenth pond is placed on the floor centered to the wall. Each pond is rendered in the mud from the bottom of the pond it represents.

  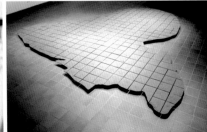 

The Garden, 1992–1997

The artist uncovers both the urban and the natural history in The Garden to reveal the physical memory in this site—all the different layers and boundaries. The garden represents a vignette of past times within the framework of contemporary Pittsburgh, like the archeological sites in Rome and Jerusalem.

Reclamation Garden, 1996

Two faces of the landscape, one formal, one rustic…

A stone tower, a Red Oak portal, and a dead fall mound speak of an internal familiarity between the space and its designer. Here the artist's sensitivities to her surroundings provided a structure for her language to be given form. 'What has happened over the years is that I've learned that reclamation is also the transformation of decline or collapse into opportunity and structure.'

Two faces of the landscape, one formal, one rustic…

THRESHOLD/INTERFACE/TRANSITION
WHEN
, 1997

One long and low room stained in transparent ochre leads into a high square room. In the high space, the clerestory windows are the only light source; five 30-foot trees rise in sections from cast stone bases to touch ceiling beams below the windows. Surrounding the trees is a base of gold leaf bordered by cut blue stone. This field, the walls, and the trees are lit by sunlight at midday.

Echo, 1999

Endangered, 1994

Pandora, 1989

WILLIAM JACKSON MAXWELL

The public work of William J. Maxwell was largely focused on site-specific environmental issues, and aimed specifically at changing the philosophy of a culture toward the environment. His art was intended to open people to other ideas through example, symbol and image, and to gain strength until finally they wake one day and have altered their actions or perspective. ● Maxwell claimed that he was led into a re-exploration of his own history on his completion of graduate school in 1976, when he returned to Auburn, California, and started exploring his old haunts. ● He would move with his logging family from Auburn to a new camp site each spring, and encounter experiences that would give Maxwell memories to influence his creativity. 'The memories that emerged from my early childhood experiences, living and playing in the woods of northern California and digging holes to that ever elusive China, are the cornerstone of my work.' ● Maxwell described these times as a great adventure in the majestic forest, since each new site offered a distinctly different experience in the woods, and contained mysteries that inspired him for many years after. 'When I think about the rainforest, I not only think about bio diversity or global warming, I think about the loss of not being able to imaginatively explore the forest and experience its nature, to create our own stories which become part of our own personal history and essence.' ● Through art, Maxwell has tried to generate transformation—to encourage people to think and act in a certain way, 'It is like the hundredth monkey. If we get enough people thinking and acting in a way that contributes to transformation, it becomes something mysterious, moving unseen through the culture—as if generic. As it washes over our psyches, we begin to accept a new way of thinking without realizing the process has been working on us. It naturally takes over.'

ECHO, 1999

This work has been designed to reflect the research conducted at the NOAA facility. Three drops of water are released from the ceiling. These drops hit the surface of the water contained in the chambers of the suspended nautilus shell. In turn, wave patterns are created on the water that reflect patterns onto the space located below the Nautilus lens. The Nautilus, in effect, is an active water lens that creates these and other optical patterns.

ENDANGERED, 1994

ENDANGERED is a site-specific piece that focuses on issues concerning threatened and extinct animals from Florida and around the world. Each animal represents one of these categories, represented as a letter that floats in the center of the image which is actually a water reservoir. The letters spell out the words endangered, rage, anger, danger, etc.

PANDORA, 1989

In preparation for PANDORA, Maxwell read extensively about the Palace of Fine Arts and its architect, Bernard Maybeck. The faux-classical female figures placed atop the colonnade represent Pandora looking into the box from which the plagues of the world were unleashed. Maxwell decided to present the viewer with the same vantage point as the Pandora figures, offering a glimpse of the interior of the box into which they gaze.

Skydance, 1995

Cycles, 1997

Skytones, 1998

Light Passageway, 1993

Memorial Union North Courtyard, 1993

ANNA VALENTINA MURCH

Anna Valentina Murch is an artist who works primarily with the medium of light, to create places that lead the viewer on a sensory and psychological journey that measures time and provokes memory. ● She received an MA in Environmental Media from the Royal College of Art in 1973 and a graduate degree in Responsive Environment from the Architectural Association, both in London, UK. In the 1970s she developed many works and had numerous exhibitions in galleries and museums. These installations investigated the qualities of space through the use of materials that transmitted, absorbed, or reflected light. ● Since 1980 her work has been involved with designing and building large public art projects that engage complex social issues. The interactive nature of this work has begun to redefine the art audience as resource and reference, as well as receiver. ● This large-scale public work has allowed her to take her personal creative investigations to another level by widening the focus to explore the definition of place. This expanded vocabulary includes ambient elements such as light, water, sound, and plant material to create sequences of spaces that change with the seasons, and heighten awareness of the natural cycles of time. ● She has worked on numerous public projects as an individual as well as a collaborative member of design teams. In addition to her personal work as an artist, she has been involved with the creation and further development of community arts legislation that increase opportunities for artists to participate as thinkers as well as object makers. She has taught at the University of California at Berkeley, the San Francisco Art Institute, and is currently Associate Professor of Art at Mills College in Oakland, California.

SKYDANCE, 1995

SKYDANCE is a 45-minute projection of 52 color changing lights on the tented ceiling of the Great Hall in the Denver International Airport Terminal. People are invited to sit and relax. This is not a big light show, but rather an attempt to draw attention to the quality of the light in Colorado. It is a soothing subtle place to rest before or after your flight.

Cycles, 1997

An interior open-air courtyard exists beyond a lobby that can be viewed but not entered. It is not possible to see all the elements of 'Cycles' from any one point of view. Instead, each element is encountered in an unfolding sequence as one surveys the courtyard from different points, each activating its own space and leading one's attention to other elements.

SKYTONES, 1998

SKYTONES is a volume lighting work located in five 25x20-inch niches along the upper level of a shopping arcade. Inside corners of each niche are curved like a diorama case to help amplify the illusion of depth and space. The modulation of light and color within these niches enhance the atmospheric quality of the space.

LIGHT PASSAGEWAY, 1993

LIGHT PASSAGEWAY is a sequence of lightscapes and shadowboxes that illuminate the fabric of the terrain of the St. Louis Metro Link system. After the train leaves the station, passengers glimpse a 'garden light well' to the south. Sunlight filters through a canopy of existing trees to light an under-story of native flowering trees, shrubs, and ferns, introduced to make a lush green ground plane.

Memorial Union North Courtyard, 1993

Self-shading furniture of steel and perforated aluminum is scattered about the plaza. Throughout the day, these linear forms cast shadows onto themselves as well as layer the ground with changing patterns. At night the added Pistachio trees, towering wind chimes, and furniture are all lit and discretely emit a glow that gives them a lantern-like presence in the darkness, creating a magical theatrical courtyard.

Boone Sculpture Garden, 1995-2000

Beacon Overlook, 1995-2001

Lantern Bridge, 1995-2001
(Under construction)

Light Islands, 1999

JODY PINTO

Jody Pinto's Italian grandmother created extraordinary gardens. Her Irish grandfather was a glass blower. Her father was an artist/photographer who did reverse paintings on glass and designed sets for dance theater. Her mother illustrated a weekly column with her best friend for a Philadelphia newspaper. Her family of six grew up in a studio apartment on 57th Street, a theater within the 'city theater' of New York. The drama of that upbringing translated itself into concerns that have been central to her work since the early seventies. Issues of relationships between the structural body and built forms; the ability of constructed forms/spaces/materials to perform; the visceral and ethereal qualities of natural and artificial light. ● Each project builds and expands the previous body of work. Each project builds new relationships, new collaborations. The studio expands and contracts like a theater ensemble. This is part of the adventure. Each project is a 'laboratory' built upon a foundation of previous exploration. The work is a constant investigation of distinct qualities of site and the materials it dictates. The goal is to infuse daily, sometimes nondescript activity with drama. Through public interaction the works become public theater.

Boone Sculpture Garden, 1995-2000

This sculpture garden is designed to respond to students, faculty, and the community. Three forms: a Plaza, Linear Water Trough, and Amphitheater define this 'garden of activities'. The concept creates a staging ground for contemporary sculpture, installation, performance, and collaboration. Night lighting outlines the forms of the garden and path system to reveal a galaxy framed by surrounding buildings.

Beacon Overlook, 1995-2001

This work is part of a master plan and five design/construction projects to refurbish the coastal frontage of Santa Monica. The fiberglass Beacon Overlook rises 45 degrees from a platform overlooking the Palisades, providing spectacular ocean views and serving as the city gateway. Five restrooms use light as a collaborator. Sunlight drenches each stall the color of its translucent fibreglass roof while night lighting transforms them into lanterns.

Lantern Bridge, 1995-2002 (Under construction)

This is an enclosure for a 144-foot steel truss service bridge 20-feet above the lobby floor. Airplane fabric is treated over a ribbed, steel bow-frame. The frames are bolted to each side of the bridge. Interior lighting triggered by a movement sensor illuminates the wing/fin enclosure while movement casts shadows upon the fabric walls. The bridge becomes a tubular shadow and light theater.

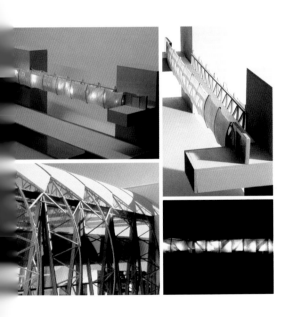

Light Islands, 1999

Six oval concrete islands represent the six municipalities of Echigo-Tsumari. Within each island a thicket of tinted fiberglass tubes of various sizes is illuminated by interior fiber-optics. At night they become lanterns. During winter the tubes cast tinted shadows on the snow. As snow rises, one sees only the fiberglass shafts of light piercing the drifts.

The Pattern that Connects, 1996

**Immigrant Desire/American Longing:
The Vestibule, 1998**

**Immigrant Desire/American Longing:
The Return, 1998**

Middle Knowledge, 1999

Kinetic Light/Air Curtain, 1993

ANTONETTE ROSATO

The public art of Antonette Rosato reflects her interest in the development of collaborative methodology and the redefining of the relationship between audience, artist, and artwork. She has worked with architects, engineers, dancers, writers, and other artists on a variety of diverse and challenging projects designed for public experience. ● The site-specific work of this artist takes advantage of many different mediums; however, she exhibits a particular interest in the experimental use of light. Light is an important tool for Rosato, who draws on its all-pervasive connection to everyday life: 'We are what we see, and yet what we see is constructed and determined, formed and transformed, by the elusive nature and often shifting character of light itself.' ● Rosato aims to use physicality, metaphor, and transformative power of light in her installations and public artwork to explore the relationship between memory and identity. Through her work, she seeks to create a 'total environment' in which the viewer is either surrounded by the work, or where the art merges with the everyday architecture of the site. Many of her pieces incorporate a participatory element that reinforces any direct engagement and further references the familiar, such as text on interior walls that can only be read by walking 'through' a piece, or video monitors in an otherwise strange environment, inclusive of visual elements often present in daily life. By framing the work within the vernacular of the 'everyday' in this way, Rosato's stated goal is to then alter that sense of familiarity, thereby challenging the viewer to consider the information in a new or different perspective, thus, creating the possibility of (re)discovery and mystery. ● 'I incite this deconstruction/expansion of the traditional figure/ground relationship between artwork and viewer, art and audience, by using light, sound, and movement to create an interactive dialogue with the people experiencing my work.'

The Pattern that Connects, 1996

Using a combination of contemporary and historical images and symbols, THE PATTERN THAT CONNECTS explores issues of contemplation, reflection, time, and memory with respect to identity. The visual interaction of Milagros, a Gnostic prayer, chiming clocks, reconstructed tools, and photo transfers of living and deceased family members, create a dialogue with the audience in this extremely complex project.

Immigrant Desire/American Longing: The Vestibule, 1998

The 'vestibule' installation suggests both masculine and feminine
qualities present in the divine. This installation takes place within
the walls of a 12th-century Gothic Chapel that is part of a former
Cistercian monastery. The two chairs in the foreground echo the
presence of both sexes in a secular sense, and visually create a
dialogue between the secular and the sacred.

IMMIGRANT DESIRE/AMERICAN LONGING: THE RETURN, 1998

(This project was a joint collaboration between Antonette Rosato and William T. Gilbert)

This is a video installation set in the attic space of a 15th-century granary, located within a former Cistercian monastery. Thematically, it was revised as the 'immigrant journey' with which many Americans and Europeans are familiar, focusing on issues of longing and desire from the past and the present, both for those immigrants who stayed behind, those who left, and those who returned.

MIDDLE KNOWLEDGE, 1999

This project was a public installation in which the artist investigated and questioned the experience of time in Western culture. Issues of domestic time, time as it exists in family memory, and the nature of divine time were explored. Beginning with objects inherited from the passing of family members, the artist created objects in response. Ultimately, the intention was to create a visual dialogue that explores our ancestral relationship to timelessness, with the belief that all things are connected and everything is related.

Kinetic Light/Air Curtain, 1993

This project utilizes chance to maintain a kind of perceptual playfulness. Propellers are used to evoke the shared metaphorical qualities indicative of both light and flight. Air is present in the movement and symbolic connections of the propellers themselves. Light is visually captured in the atmospheric qualities of flight and metaphorically evokes the meaning of light as it illuminates the way through the journey itself.

Big Bubble, 1998

O House, 1995

Tree House, 2000

Jewel, 2000

DEAN RUCK

Dean Ruck insists that his motivation and desire to make art has always been tempered by doubts as to whether society places value on, or gives validity to art and artists. This dilemma has stolen his resolve to find relevance in what he creates. Ruck has made it clear that he rejected long ago creating self-indulgent, autobiographical, or decorative art. 'I am interested in creating an existential situation for the view that involves them physically, viscerally, and psychologically'. ● Large-scale interactive installations and objects in the environment allow the viewer to enter into a symbiotic relationship with the art. As such, meaning is as much about the shared space of art and viewer as it is about any specific intention of the artist. As metaphor, this is congruent with what connects each of us: shared space, common experience, sensory perception, and animal instinct. 'Creating a situation for reaction, interaction, wonderment, and fascination can, hopefully, function as a catalyst for real experience synonymous with our experience of everyday life when we are lost in our thoughts or too aware of our actions'. ● Ruck has also said that on another level, what he does is simple indulgence and affirmation of ego. Being able to work with one's hands and body as tools to create, to transform space and materials, to leave a mark, gives the fulfilment of being alive and feeling part of the world. As a child of nature, he says he is bound to its subtle and grand phenomena and beauty. 'Nature is the standard by which I measure the effect of my art'.

Big Bubble, 1998

Big Bubble is a tribute to the 'common man' with three interactive artworks. 'Site Seeing' is the representation of 15 decades in the history of the people of Houston. 'Sounds from the Past' recreates the sounds of a steamship on Buffalo Bayou in remembrance of the city's *raison d'être*. It is activated by passing pedestrians and at timed intervals. Big Bubble is intended as an element of surprise, wonderment, and fascination for park visitors, as well as a device to activate and aerate the slow moving water. It will remind visitors of a bayou, or living ecological system that is ever changing and teeming with life and history. Big Bubble confounds, perplexes, and startles the unexpecting pedestrian as a vigorous burst of air rises from the floor of the bayou and dissipates into far reaching ripples along the surface of the water. An automatic timer and a publicly accessible push button activate the Big Bubble.

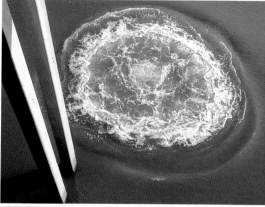

O House, 1995

Ruck joined Kate Petley, and Dan Havel to create a phenomenological installation which brings the primordial elements of earth, sky, and water within the untouchable reach of the viewer. They turned an old house into an exploratorium of the senses. The exterior was left with boarded up windows, peeling paint, city citations, and graffiti, while the interior was completely gutted and restructured into a circular, spiraling oasis of light, sound and touch. The viewer's notion of interior is obliterated by eight yards of dirt covering the floor and the diminishing light level. When the visitor's eyes adjust they become witnesses of constantly fluctuating images of trees, clouds, birds, and even lightning if lucky enough. Streaks of light beam through two-foot holes punched into the floor, creating a large camera obscura, while also illuminating a central subterranean pool of water.

 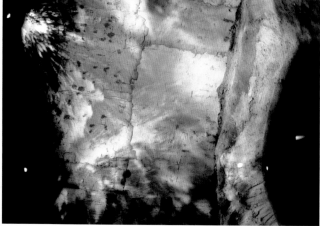 

TREE HOUSE, 2000

TREE HOUSE consists of a nearly-complete tree, covered with encaustic wax and suspended vertically inside a house, creating a paradoxical dialectic between our conventional notion of inside verses outside, vertical verses horizontal, and man verses nature. The trunk juts from the floor vertically in the corner of the house, then makes an abrupt 90-degree turn and fills the interior space with its branches and limbs. The viewer can enter the house and navigate through the branches, judging its weight, the logistics of its placement, and the peculiarity of the myriad of juxtapositions.

JEWEL, 2000

JEWEL is a collaborative outdoor project by Dean Ruck and Debbie McNulty, which is installed at a nature conservatory called Connemara, outside Dallas, Texas. The mission of Connemara becomes increasingly critical with typical urban sprawl spreading like wild fire around it. In ten years Connemara has gone from being a section of the beautiful Texas prairie and Pecan groves to a 72-acre island surrounded by planned communities and commercial development. The artists wanted to celebrate and honor this refuge by placing a jewel in the landscape. The sculpture consists of a 16-foot spherical steel armature covered with various size tree branches wrapped in copper foil. The reflective quality of the copper foil is responsive to the changing sunlight.

Dallas Convention Center Expansion
Project, 1993

Biochemistry Waltz, 1998

Brief Cases, 1998

Courthouse Station, 2000

Gallivan Plaza Light Rail Station, 2000

NORIE SATO

Norie Sato's concerns as an artist are often involved with connections between nature and technology. Issues of transition, edges, and memory play an important role within the larger construct. She has worked with electronics, especially video, for a number of years. The electronic image, the nature of technology and the juxtaposition of the analog and digital inform her work even if the medium used is of a completely different nature. In the studio, she works with plate glass, cutting and hand etching it in combination with other materials. She has also utilized photographic or video images, as well as images processed by computer. ● The combination of the technological with the hand-made, the machine-made and the human touch is something she has been pursuing for a number of years. She grew up in a science-oriented family, with a physicist father, a mathematician brother, and scientists on both grandparent sides. Thus the combination of art, science, and technology has always been at the core of her interest. ● Though she brings her artistic concerns to bear for public artworks, she also brings in ideas specifically related to aspects of the site and its function: historical, cultural, sociological, and physical as well as the human touch and scale. Through a combination of visual imagery and text, with an idea based in the place itself, she aims to create public art which is timeless and helps inject a site with a sense of place, purpose, discovery, and wonder. ● She utilizes a variety of different media in her public work: glass, steel, cast bronze, and other metals, terrazzo, landscaping concepts, and light, for example. She works first with ideas, then with the medium, selecting the appropriate manifestation of her idea for the context.

DALLAS CONVENTION CENTER EXPANSION PROJECT, 1993

This collaboration between Norie Sato, William J. Maxwell,
Garrison Roots, and Phillip Lamb, used imagery derived from
the Dallas region. The ground level focused on elements
natural to Dallas, sprinkled with cultural references,
captured in the shape of a snake and numerous 'fossilized'
images of local culture, flora, and fauna. On the exhibit level,
the images, while still Dallas-based, became somewhat
more abstract, metaphorical, metaphysical or celestially
related.

Biochemistry Waltz, 1998

This terrazzo floor contains images based on biochemistry, primarily the hexagon and pentagon, which are both molecular structures. Students and faculty provided source material and some terrazzo strip inlays about protein ribbons, RNA, DNA, antibodies, and viruses that weave through the hexagonal base. Vitamin D, an important compound within the historical and current research at the university, is also prominently placed.

Brief Cases, 1998

This collaboration between Norie Sato, Tad Savinar, and Bill Will, sited on the curved wall outside Portland City Council Chambers, addresses the intersection between the civic and the personal. Twenty-eight cast-bronze assemblages of miniature and life-size objects expressing the personal, and 29 stainless steel plates with text and images expressing the civic, are placed on different grids, creating varying relationships between the two systems.

COURTHOUSE STATION, 2000

The elements contained here refer to the balance of decisions needed to keep a city alive. Six cast-bronze seats are formed in the shape of weights which might be used with the symbolic balance hanging from the OCS pole. Each object refers to a transformation, a duality, or a relationship such as leaves turning into a book. Several hundred names have been sandblasted into the windscreen in reference to the importance of family and individual.

GALLIVAN PLAZA LIGHT RAIL STATION, 2000

The notion of 'place' is central to this work. Facts about the community, culture, and geography were placed in cast bronze 'X' shapes, inlaid into the platform. Seats of carved Utah sandstone taper downward to point to place and emphasize the link between the physical and the temporal place of the 'here and now', and the future. Cast-bronze crickets indicate the benefits of the natural world and the threat of too many insects against a growing population.

120

BROWARD COUNTY

HOUSTON

MIAMI-DADE

SAN FRANCISCO

SAN DIEGO

MTA METRO ART

PHOENIX

SAN JOSE

ART PROGRAMS

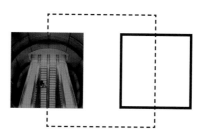

Accordant Zones, 1994

Calypso, 1998

Everglades Tresspass, 2000

Light Cylinders, 1996-2001

BROWARD COUNTY
CULTURAL AFFAIRS COUNCIL

The Broward County Public Art and Design Program allocates two percent to commissioned artists to provide design expertise, and to create artworks within a broad range of capital improvement projects. The purpose of the program is to contribute to the enhancement of urban design through the creation of commissioned works of art that create a sense of place, that improve the visual environment for the citizens of Broward County, and that advance the missions of the county departments where the projects reside. Commissioned artworks are the result of a dynamic interaction between selected artists and interested constituent groups during the design stages of the projects. ● The Broward County Art in Public Places Program was established in 1978 for the purpose of enhancing the county's heritage and promoting a greater understanding and awareness of the visual arts. ● Artists are now commissioned at the early design stages of a project so that they may effectively collaborate with the architect as a member of the project design team. Artists are encouraged to reach out to the community in the early stages of the design process to ensure that the resulting artworks and aesthetic amenities respond to community needs and perceptions. ● The committee which oversees the operation of the program recommends the appointment of seven specialized selection panels. The selection process, which includes community and agency representatives, is intended to promote excellence while ensuring fairness, diversity, and sensitivity to the specific needs of constituent groups.

ACCORDANT ZONES, 1994/BARBARA NEIJNA & NED SMYTH

ACCORDANT ZONES is an expansive sculptural park built to provide an elegant and relaxed outdoor greenery for its office workers and visitors to the downtown area. The park includes three large sculptural structures, a Sphere, Disc, and Cone, which are visually connected by seating walls and walkways. With diverse materials of steel, concrete, olitic limestone, and lush tropical landscaping, the park creates a unique setting for the visual enhancement of the judicial complex and the downtown New River. The setting gives the viewer a sense of lushness and a monumentality, which resonate a sense of awe and harmony with those who use it.

Calypso, 1998/Tobey Archer

Archer retrofitted the interior of an old cargo terminal at Fort Lauderdale's

Port Everglades for new use by the cruise industry. Located adjacent to a

convention center, terminal two lacked ambience. To enhance passenger

embarkation and debarkation, she choreographed an engaging dance of

color and light. She developed a great hall, which established a sense of

tropical place, and pleasant expectations suitable for Caribbean-bound

passengers. The artist playfully and skillfully choreographed a mile of

fiber-optic cable on the ceiling of the great hall, unifying the immense open

space. To provide a more intimate feeling within the cavernous hall,

Archer developed a palette of warm painted gem tones, such as mango

and canton jade for use on the walls, doors, and columns, completing the

transformation of the industrial space.

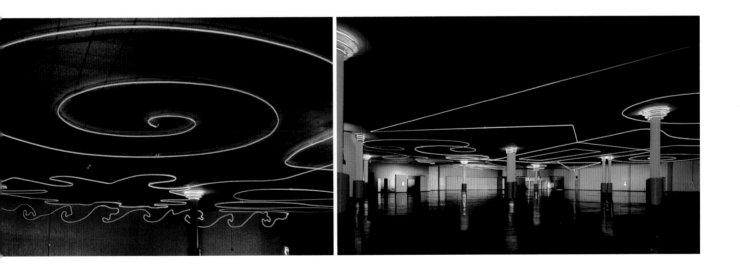

Everglades Tresspass, 2000/Carl Cheng

Cheng chose the water and light features of South Florida as a common theme from community input he had gathered. The terrazzo floor design is a perception map of Florida, from the Everglades through the canal system and suburbanization to the beach. Elements of the piece include a terrazzo floor reflecting the natural landscape. Its water, grasses, alligators, a dividing roadway, and two art glass skylights, reflect the brilliant hues and whites of the fast moving clouds and watery landscape.

Light Cylinders, 1996-2001/Jody Pinto

Housing escalators, four 88x34-foot fiberglass cylinders rise through all floors of the garage and are canopied by translucent tensile fabric structures. Serving as locator and facilitator, these solar/lunar lanterns of various colors are events of light and movement. Passengers become part of this interior spectacle as they move through the cylinders.

CITY OF SAN DIEGO COMMISSION FOR ART AND CULTURE

Metro Biosolids Center, 1998

The Alvarado Garden, 1998

Balboa Park, 1997

When the City of San Diego commits to building and renovation projects, it commits to reform and renewal of the city by carefully planning the way a facilty looks, operates, and relates to the community. The City of San Diego Commission for Art and Culture's Public Art Program has transformed San Diego's built environment by making the artist an integral participant in public planning and design. Since the program began in 1988, more than 80 public art projects have been initiated. The public art program oversees the maintenance and restoration of the city's collection of historic and contemporary artworks. ● San Diego has pioneered an innovative and dynamic approach to public art. Its public art policy allows each department to select capital improvement projects for artist involvement on a case by case basis. It is a flexible process that adapts easily to the unique circumstances of each design and construction project.

METRO BIOSOLIDS CENTER, 1998/RICHARD TURNER

This work was designed to address both visitors and employees at the biosolids plant. The artist employed images, text and three-dimensional forms to clearly communicate information about the process and the facility. The METRO BIOSOLIDS CENTER integrates landscaping, architecture, and art to provide an overall unity. The intrigue of working with a cultural taboo and the challenge of making difficult information accessible proved a fascinating opportunity for the artist. The entire facility challenges the standard approach to the design of a public facility by creating an educational and aesthetic experience.

THE ALVARADO GARDEN, 1998/ROBERT MILLAR

The artist studied the local environment and the water treatment facilities to make a visit
to the reservoir both educational and aesthetically pleasing. Visitors approaching the
reservoir pass through a grove of sycamore trees, which are generally associated with
water. The reservoir is accessed via a wood-planked walkway, which has been hand-
branded with 5,000 words that pose questions about the history and use of water.
THE ALVARADO GARDEN allows spectacular views of Lake Murray, the dam, and the canyon
below the lake.

BALBOA PARK, 1997/CINDY ZIMMERMAN

This project exists on an inactive landfill in the East Mesa portion of Balboa Park. The exposition included temporary earthworks, adobe sculptures, and public events, all designed for community involvement. The site, formerly a network of canyon fingers and arroyos leading to the Florida canyon fault, was first filled with trash from the expositions of 1915 and 1935. Innovative dumping lead to standard land filling techniques from the 1950s through to 1974. The Arizona Street Landfill, as it was called by the City of San Diego, was the official repository of household refuse from the city. The former canyon, now a broad mesa, was to be kept open to the sky, to return to native non-protected vegetation, and to be accessed via nature trails.

Countree Music, 1999

Seven Wonders, 1998

Elevator Core, 2000

Metro Bus Shelter, 1999

CULTURAL ARTS COUNCIL OF HOUSTON

The Civic Art and Design program initiates and manages civic enhancement projects in the Houston / Harris County region. The program serves as a community resource and works, on a consulting basis, with both public and private sector entities. To date the program has leveraged over US$2.8 million in capital construction and artist fees. Outreach and information resources include an ongoing series of lectures and workshops on public art and urban design, a public art library, and a registry of artists and their work. ● Houston is rightfully proud of its public art program and the recognition it has received, crediting its success to the talented and ambitious artists involved with the program. The strength of their vision and professional tenacity has given to the city an influx of exciting new artworks through its short history. ● Accordingly, since late 1994, CACHH's Civic Art and Design program has worked with various city departments, as well as other government entities such as METRO, on a series of pilot projects to demonstrate the benefits of including artists in the design of public infrastructure. Due to the success of these efforts, CACHH is now seeking to institutionalize this approach and to make civic art and design a permanent part of the city's development. The most effective means to accomplish this goal is to strengthen or replace the council resolution with an ordinance that mandates the inclusion of civic art and design into all of the City of Houston's building projects.

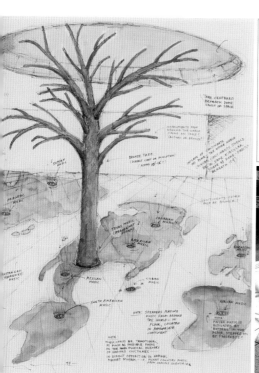

COUNTREE MUSIC, 1999/TERRY ALLEN

The work's centerpiece is a bronze casting of a 25-foot oak tree, selected from a ranch near Splendora, Texas. Passengers are serenaded by 18 original songs composed by Allen, fellow Texas music great Joe Ely, and former Talking Head David Byrne. Travelers crossing the terrazzo map on the floor that completes this piece see that on this map, Houston is the center of the world. Allen said that the installation gives travelers 'the experience of actually being able to move around inside the heart of a song'.

SEVEN WONDERS, 1998/MEL CHIN

The artist collaborated with 1,050 schoolchildren, and the architects of the Wortham Center, which is home to the world-renowned ballet and opera companies of Houston. What looks like lace from a distance is actually laser-cut stainless steel. Chin asked schoolchildren born in 1986, Houston's sesquicentennial year, to submit drawings depicting each of the seven themes: agriculture, energy, manufacturing, medicine, philanthropy, technology, and transportation. Selecting 150 for each pillar, he and artists Rachael Splinter and Helen Nagge translated each drawing into a computer image, which was then laser cut into stainless steel. These projections of the city's present character came from the generation that will form its future.

ELEVATOR CORE, 2000/RACHEL HECKER

The artist integrated the artwork of the elevator core as a seamless component of the terminal upgrade. Beginning on the ITT level, stainless-steel wall cladding and cobalt blue lighting ascend to the ticket lobby. As an interior 'first point of entry' the core is not only a vertical transport system, but a progression from a quiet, dark, carpeted, low-ceiling, below-grade spatial experience on the ITT level to a highly active, bright, multi-functional, civic-scaled lobby. At the ticket lobby the stainless steel wraps the elevator shaft in the shape of a Chinese lantern. The design changes the profile of the elevator shaft, draws the eye upward and transforms the experience of moving up and into an attenuated space.

Metro Bus Shelter, 1999/Rachel Hecker, Benito Huerta, & Richard Turner

Lorenzo Thomas was chosen to incorporate poetry into the streets in this collaboration between artists and design firms. Excerpts of poetry by generations of Texas poets was etched into sidewalk pavers in a work called Texts in Contexts. The art enhancements developed as part of this extensive street improvement project include unique sidewalk paving and inlays, seating, and enhancements to the new bus shelter.

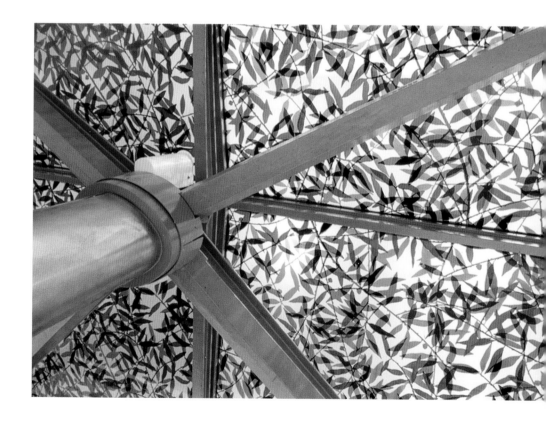

I Dreamed I Could Fly, 1993

Vermont/Santa Monica Station, 1999

People Coming/People Going, 1996

Crenshaw/I-105 Station, 1995

MTA METRO ART

Recognizing that art can bring a touch of humanity to an often mundane commute, MTA commissions artists to incorporate art into a wide array of transportation projects. From bus stops to rail stations, streetscapes to bus interiors, construction fences to poetry, art creates a sense of place and instills pride in communities. ● Known for its interdisciplinary approach as well as the broad range of artists who have been commissioned, Metro Art is also recognized for its innovative and successful community and corporate contributions. Metro Art has established a Docent Program, which offers free group tours led by knowledgeable volunteer docents. ● **Metro Rail** MTA policy allocates 0.5 percent of the rail construction costs to the enhancement of the rail system through the arts. Artists, design professionals, and community members are brought together in the design process of the rail transit facilities and construction mitigation programs. ● **Metro Bus** Metro Art has initiated a number of art projects which enhance the transit experience for over one million Metro Bus customers daily. Projects have included a series of photo essay bus cards, live poetry readings, collectible bookmarks, art enhancements to the customer service/ticket centers, and artist-designed monthly/weekly passes. ● **Streetscapes** Artists are participating in demonstration projects for bus stop enhancements as well as a number of other pedestrian oriented projects, including a major pedestrian bridge in downtown Los Angeles. ● **Metrolink** For those cities in LA County interested in enhancing their Metrolink station with art, Metro Art coordinates a matching grant program.

I DREAMED I COULD FLY, 1993/JONATHAN BOROFSKY

These sculptures are made of recognizable forms—humans, clowns, animals—used in a playful manner and unusual context to provoke diverse interpretations. 'I've had quite a few flying dreams in my lifetime. Many other people I've spoken to have had similar dreams. Sometimes I fly above it all, serene and rather enlightened…other times my flying dreams seem more like an escape from earthly concerns.' In a reflection of the universal motif of flight as a spiritual journey, Jonathan Borofsky's I DREAMED I COULD FLY is an interpretation of the artist's dreams of flying. The six fiberglass figures, all resembling the artist, soar and cast large shadows in the high bay area of Civic Center Station. The work has an audible element as well—an occasional trill of a bird accompanies the figures.

Vermont/Santa monica Station, 1999/Robert Millar

The question is the foundation of intellectual inquiry. The question helps us to identify the relationship between cultural, social, and economic issues. The question helps us to identify what a project like this is actually about, and what we may learn from it. The artist sees his work as performance art.

People Coming/People Going, 1996/Richard Wyatt

The artist is a noted muralist, and known for his realistic figurative works, which honor both common people and historic people. He is interested in connecting with people through art, and in this work, helping people connect with the idea of how important they are to making the city—and mass transit—work. Most of the finished tiles had to be fired and re-fired many times to obtain the variety of color and depth required. It was a very slow process. Wyatt has designed two 52-foot-long ceramic murals for the end walls of the Wilshire/Western Station. People Coming presents portraits of members of the community as they approach the viewer; People Going shows some members of that group walking away. Portions of the famous Wiltern Theater, located just across from the station entrance, can be seen in the background.

CRENSHAW/I-105 STATION, 1995/BUZZ SPECTOR

Spector's work uses the book as subject and object for inquiry into the relationship between history and memory, and of the library as a metaphor for both. 'Transportation systems are not just means of moving people—they are metaphors of the cultural and spiritual links between peoples. CRENSHAW STORIES has been designed to stress the connections between us that may be found in stories we tell about our lives. If we can better understand each other's stories, we'll be better able to appreciate the connections between us all.' The work uses collected stories from station-area residents in several languages, including Spanish, Korean, Japanese, Chinese, Thai, Arabic, Russian, and Tagalog. Seventy-two of these stories were hand painted onto tile and interspersed with color tiles at the entrance of the station. In addition, 72 of the most commonly spoken languages by children in Los Angeles public schools, each coupled with the word 'American,' are embedded at intervals across the platform.

A Walk on the Beach Phase 1, 1995

36th Street Wall, 1996

Harmonic Runway, 1995

Aqua Botanica, 1997

MIAMI-DADE ART IN PUBLIC PLACES

The Art in Public Places program of Miami-Dade is one of the oldest percent-for-art programs in the United States. It was established in 1973 and gave Miami pioneer status in public art programming, enlarging and enhancing the public design process. ● The city has established an allocation for works of art based on 1.5 percent of the construction cost of new county buildings. The goals of the program are several: to enhance artistic heritage, to give dimension to the public environment for residents and visitors, increase public awareness of the works of art, and to promote an awareness and understanding of the visual arts. ● The program has commissioned over 500 works to date and gained international recognition. Artworks are installed throughout Miami-Dade at transit stations, Miami International Airport, fire and police stations, public housing developments, Metro Zoo, community health centers, and other public facilities which form a part of the Miami-Dade family of services to the community. ● The latest focus of the program has been on site-specific, collaborative projects. Some involve artists, landscape architects, historians, engineers, and architects in a team approach. Creative problem solving through innovative collaboration has resulted in projects that validate, define, and expand community identity. ● An innovative educational component develops programming for the youth of their community. The county supports the development of a unique and vital civic environment though its art in public places program.

A WALK ON THE BEACH PHASE 1, 1995/MICHELE OKA DONER

Long walks along Miami's beaches observing shells, seaweed, and other marine forms deposited by the tides inspired this monumental site-specific art installation. Phase I of A Walk on the Beach, a half-mile-long walkway featuring two thousand unique cast-bronze elements embedded in a dark gray terrazzo matrix, celebrates the saltwater plants and vertebrate creatures inhabiting South Florida's shallow coastal waters. Scatterings of mother-of-pearl create a richness of texture and reference the sea foam at the water's edge.

36TH STREET WALL/MARTHA SCHWARTZ

Schwartz is an artist/landscape architect. Her work explores the relationship between art, culture, and landscape in many site-specific art installations. This sound attenuation wall, fabricated from reinforced concrete pierced by colored glass discs, was designed to create visual appeal to motorists. Inspired by jet aviation control panels, Schwartz randomly placed the translucent colored discs throughout the mile-long undulating wall.

HARMONIC RUNWAY, 1995/CHRISTOPHER JANNEY

Tropical colors, sounds of the Everglades, and intense light enliven HARMONIC RUNWAY, an interactive sound and light environment created by artist/composer Christopher Janney. This 180-foot-long space is composed of 132 sheets of vividly colored glass, each 10 feet tall, ranging from deep violet to bright red, and a sound-score based on the natural environments of South Florida. Moving through the zones of color, one may hear distant crickets, frogs, or a flock of birds flying over the Everglades. Travelers passing through the artwork activate photo-electric cells which trigger sounds of melodic instruments. The forms and phenomena of HARMONIC RUNWAY attempt to reveal an essence, an 'abstraction' of South Florida through color and sound.

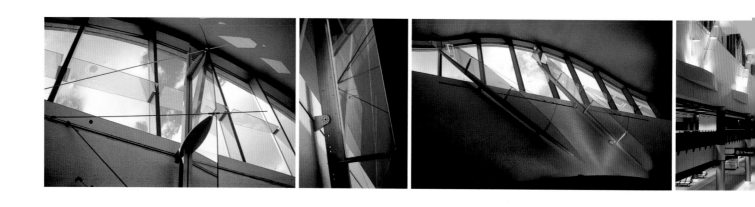

AQUA BOTANICA, 1997/ED CARPENTER, MIKE McCULLOCH

The artists collaborated with architect Mike McCulloch, and artist John Rogers to develop a visual system in progressions of interval line and color to lead travelers through the concourse and unify the space. Their collaboration is ambiguous, abstractly evoking images of fantastic flying machines, exotic botanical species, and dreamlike submarine environments.

Papago Park/City Boundry, 1992

An Open Book, 1996

The Grasshopper Bridge, 1997

Paradise Lane Bridge, 1998

Nisbet Road Pedestrian Bridge, 1998

PHOENIX ARTS COMMISSION

The Public Art Program was established in 1986 through an ordinance that allocates up to one percent of the city's capital improvement program to public art. Art projects are funded through the sale of bonds which are repaid with revenue from the city's secondary property tax and enterprise funds. Each year, the arts commission works with the other city departments to develop an annual public art program which identifies capital improvement projects in all areas of the city which offer the greatest opportunity for artist involvement and public accessibility. The plan is presented to city council for review and approval. ● The community also participates in the program. Neighborhood meetings are held where projects are being developed to provide opportunities for the community to meet the artist and express its values, memories, and visions. The best public art emerges from a meeting of minds and spirits. ● The Phoenix Arts Commission's public art program provides opportunities for artists to create artworks to enhance public spaces, and to work with architects, engineers, landscape architects, and city planners to design and build neighborhood parks, community centers, bridges, plazas, streets, recycling centers, and other important civic amenities. Phoenix is living, evolving proof of how public art helps create a more beautiful and distinctive city.

Papago Park/City Boundary, 1992/Jody Pinto

Pinto's approach to the project centers on Papago Park's identity as a major historical and ecological boundary, as well as an entrance to the park. The design consists of seven 16-foot-high markers along a 240-foot-wall with seven branches radiating from its center symbolising a tree of life. The piece is made from stacked and mortared field stone in a manner similar to the park's historical ramadas. The markers serve as axes for directing viewers to municipal, historical, and natural sites in the valley. They also align with the summer solstice. The wall structure, which forms the stem of the plant, functions as a water harvesting device and aqueduct. Run off from summer storms is captured and diverted through a channel in the wall onto each of the seven farming terraces, which are planted with native plants.

An Open Book, 1996/Mayme Kratz, Debra L. Hopkins, Valerie Vadala Homer

An Open Book is a collaborative effort that focuses on the primary building blocks of our language and learning systems. Fifty-six blocks of amber resin gently curve along a glass wall. Individually cast, each block contains natural and found objects, as well as fragments of poetry and texts. Through the incorporation of significant text with the objects, the artists emphasize to the viewer the importance of literacy and learning, encouraging participants to explore the limitless resources housed in the library. Embodying the spirit of imagination, An Open Book encourages people of all ages to view the importance of literacy and learning.

  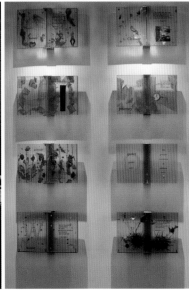

THE GRASSHOPPER BRIDGE, 1997/ED CARPENTER

Carpenter's approach from the start was to seek imagery which captures the imagination of the young users. Mindful that the quality of the passage through the bridge is as important as the view of it from the surroundings, the artist arrived at solutions which are as exciting in cross section as they are in elevation. Budgetary constraints made this a special challenge. The artist worked with staff from the Phoenix Street Transportation Department and the Phoenix Arts Commission, as well as a local engineer, to design a 9x210-foot crossing which connects two parks. It is used primarily by school children whose passage is occasionally blocked by high water from the wash beneath. The bridge is highly visible from 7th Avenue, a busy feeder street.

PARADISE LANE BRIDGE, 1998/LINNEA GLATT

The PARADISE LANE BRIDGE spans State Highway 51, providing safe passageway for pedestrian and bicycle traffic between residential areas on either side. The bridge cover, a visually elaborate woven basket-like structure, suggests a kind of reweaving of the two sides of the neighborhood. Travelers experience the interior as an intriguing play of light and shadow. The 'basket' cover is woven from galvanized metal strips, which are perforated at the bottom while the top half remains solid.

NISBET ROAD PEDESTRIAN BRIDGE, 1998/LAURIE LUNDQUIST

The NISBET ROAD PEDESTRIAN BRIDGE spans State Highway 51, providing a safe passageway for pedestrian and bicycle traffic between the residential areas on the other side. This 260-foot-bridge spans east and west, establishing a physical link to the north and south bicycle path on the west side of the highway. Conceptually, Lundquist draws a visual link with the mountain vistas to the south and the bridge's profile, echoing the distant jagged peaks. The bridge also includes a safety cage made from small-weave galvanized chain link.

Functional and Fantasy Stair, Cyclone
Fragment, 1996

Constellation, 1996

Jury Assembly Room,1997-98

Civic Center Court House Entry Doors.
Security Gates, and Door Handles, 1997-98

Untitled, 1996

SAN FRANCISCO
ARTS COMMISSION

San Francisco's public art program, one of the first in the United States, was established in 1969. An ordinance provides that two percent of construction costs of civic buildings, transportation improvement projects, new parks, and other aboveground structures such as bridges, is to be allocated for public art. It also provides an allowance for artwork conservation projects. The public art program seeks to promote a diverse and stimulating cultural environment to enrich the lives of the city residents, visitors, and employees. The program encourages the creative interaction of artists, designers, city staff, officials, and community members during the design of city projects, in order to develop public art that is specific and meaningful to the site and to the community. Public art is developed and implemented in conjunction with the overall design and construction of each project. Each project's life span from the design phase through completion of construction is approximately three to seven years.

Functional and Fantasy Stair, Cyclone Fragment, 1996/Alice Aycock

Mysterious stairways symbolise knowledge in this work. A functional spiral stair wraps around a tipped cone, which in turn wraps around a column. It appears to be unraveling itself. As it unravels, fragments of false or imaginary stairs peel off. A second sculpture, Cyclone Fragment, is suspended in the adjacent atrium space above the fourth floor, functioning as a ghost projection of the spiral stair. If the spiral stair suggests knowledge unfolding, Cyclone Fragment suggests knowledge in the most dynamic and transitional state. In addition to metaphorical allusions of the sculptures to the uses of the library, there is a formal relationship to the building as well. The form of both artworks is a sculptural response to the conical design of the building's great atrium skylight, used elsewhere in the building as a decorative motif.

CONSTELLATION, 1996/NAYLAND BLAKE

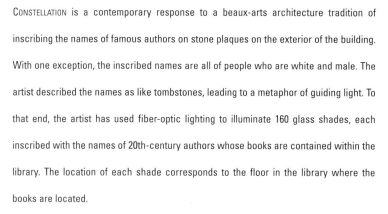

CONSTELLATION is a contemporary response to a beaux-arts architecture tradition of inscribing the names of famous authors on stone plaques on the exterior of the building. With one exception, the inscribed names are all of people who are white and male. The artist described the names as like tombstones, leading to a metaphor of guiding light. To that end, the artist has used fiber-optic lighting to illuminate 160 glass shades, each inscribed with the names of 20th-century authors whose books are contained within the library. The location of each shade corresponds to the floor in the library where the books are located.

JURY ASSEMBLY ROOM, 1997-98/LEWIS DESOTO

JURY ASSEMBLY ROOM features eight sand-blasted glass panels. Each end panel is a close up depiction of a section of the US Constitution. One set of panels depicts an empty room, the other a room full of people with their identities removed. The reflective qualities of the glass allows the potential for the participant to take the place of an august member of the founders of the US government, thus symbolically carrying the tradition of living participation in the law. People walking in the hallway leading to the jury room pass through a projected light image of the California state symbol.

CIVIC CENTER COURT HOUSE ENTRY DOORS, SECURITY GATES, AND DOOR HANDLES, 1997-98/ALBERT PALEY

These works are both an artistic adornment of the building as well as functional components. The front door handles, sandblasted glass panels of the front doors, five pairs of lobby security gates, the pattern which has been etched onto the surface of the elevator doors, and the brackets within the elevator cab which support the hand railings, have all been designed by the artist. The work provides a magic sense of arrival and entry, allowing elements of the exterior architecture to be subtly incorporated into the interior design.

Untitled, 1996/Ann Hamilton & Ann Chamberlain

This work was created in homage to libraries of the past, and in this case, as a tribute to the old catalog card reference system, and spans three levels of the principal wall in the library. The new library and the transition to an on-line catalog made manilla cards artefacts. The interest of the artist lies in the change of technology from the physical experience of the card catalogs and system to the electronic and visual on-line system. Together with 200 scribes, they hand annotated 50,000 old library catalog cards in a dozen different languages, with quotes either from books or references to related books.

Origin, 1999

Untitled, 1999

Jump Cuts, 1996

SAN JOSE PUBLIC ART PROGRAM

Like many cities, suburban flight of the fifties and early sixties left San Jose's once active downtown with boarded-up storefronts, vacant office buildings, and urban blight. The late seventies and early eighties saw the creation of a new downtown through extensive urban renovation efforts. The city took on the task of creating a new downtown—one that included retail, housing, entertainment, office development, and public spaces. To support renovation efforts, the city passed a one-percent-for-art ordinance in 1984 that set aside a percentage of capital improvement project budgets for artwork. The intent of the public art program was to enhance the new downtown with purchased works of art, located in, or adjacent to new facilities in the city center. ● To date, the Public Art Program has completed 46 projects in city parks, libraries, municipal and recreational facilities, parking garages, and through neighborhood-initiated public art projects. Projects have ranged in budget size from US$7,000 to multi-millions. Today, the public art program has a full-time staff of five who manage an average of 38 projects per year, with an annual budget of approximately US$6 million.

ORIGIN, 1999/BRAD GOLDBERG, BELIZ BROTHER, & JOSEPH MCSHANE

Set in the south atrium space of the Tech Museum of Innovation, a cylindrical tower-structure becomes part of an overall composition that encompasses the floor of the atrium, the walls, and the entire volume of space. A gilded nine-foot diameter tower sits within the open atrium space and rises 45 feet from the lower level. A bold yet simple form is created in an already architecturally dynamic space, and a visual link is made between the three levels of the museum. Upon first glance the tower sculpture appears to be a traditional sculptural object within an architectural space, but upon further study and exploration, the tower reveals itself to be much more. This project explores the relationship between art and technology, and celebrates the earth's basic natural resources which, when manipulated through imagination, create innovation.

UNTITLED, 1999/ANN CHAMBERLAIN, AND VICTOR MARIO ZABALLA

The main theme of the artwork is Cemanahuac, which is known as the location of the individual within their community and the cosmos. Gates into the plaza use symbols to represent one of the four cardinal elements. Mosaic thresholds inside the gates incorporate images relating to fire, wind, earth, and water. Garden alcoves are offering places; each linked by thematic press tiles that were created by the community during a series of public workshops. The photographic tiles were translated from family albums and personal photographic collections from the local community. The hummingbird is a recurring image within the garden, and the plantings in the garden are intended to attract hummingbirds which are an ancient Meso-American talisman; a symbol of love and the warrior spirit, and are common in San Jose. A hummingbird motif is intended to speak to the spirit of San Jose's immigrant citizens.

JUMP CUTS, 1996/ELIZABETH DILLER & RICARDO SCOFIDIO, WITH PAUL LEWIS

The movie marquee became a familiar downtown architectural feature with the popularization of cinema in the 1920s and 1930s. Its objective of transmitting information to the street was fully realized at night with illuminated displays as a form of urban seduction. A contemporary interpretation of the marquee suggests not only technical revision for this transmission of information, but a rethinking of urban communication. JUMP CUTS reinterprets the mechanism of the marquee through sculptural, electronic and video elements, broadcasting images and texts, both informational and contemplative, to the street. The artwork transforms the visual accessibility of the lobby by alternating between the actual view from the street and live video views from within, thus flipping the building inside out and back, electronically. By day, viewers see text permanently etched onto the surface of the glass panels. From the outside, the text reads, 'Truth is stranger than fiction is stranger than truth...'. From inside the lobby, the text reads, 'Life imitates art imitates life...'.

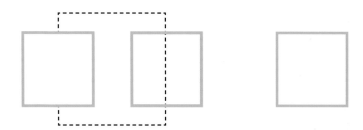

GENERAL CREDITS

ARTISTS

TERRY ALLEN   18

19   **Notre Denver**, 1994 (Architect: Fentress Bradburn & Associates, Commissioned by the Public Art Program of the City
       and County of Denver), Denver International Airport, Denver, Colorado, USA

20   **Modern Communication**, 1995 (Commissioning agency: Kansas City Arts Commission), New Police and Fire Department
       Communication Center, Kansas City, Missouri, USA

21   **Corporate Head**, 1990 (Commissioning agency: Seventh Street Plaza Associates), City Corps Plaza, Poets Walk,
       Los Angeles, California, USA

23   **Belief**, 1999 (Architect: Frank O. Gehry, Commissioning agency: Ohio Arts Council), Vontz Center for Molecular Research,
       University of Cincinati, Cincinnati, Ohio, USA

JOAN LLAVERIA ARASA   24

25   **Line 3 of Valencia's Subway**, 1999 (Commissioning agency: Ministerio de Obras Publicas),
       Estacion Hermanos Machado, Valencia, Spain

27   **Sculptural Garden of Font del riu**, 1999 (Commissioning agency: Gobierno Local), Central Park, Gata de Gorgos, Alicante, Spain

29   **Cultural Center**, "La Asuncion", 1998, Albacete, Spain

30   **Gran Caribe Hotel**, (Commissioning agency: CODEMA) Cayolargo del Sur, Cuba

ED CARPENTER   32

33   **Market Street Pedestrian Bridge**, 2001 (Commissioning agency: City of San Antonio), San Antonio Convention Center,
       San Antonio, Texas, USA

35   **Flying Bridge**, 1998 (Architect: The Tsang Partnership, Commissioning agency: Central Washington University and
       Washington State Arts Commssion), The Dean Science Building Central Washington University, 400E. 8th Avenue,
       Ellensburg, Washington, USA

36   **Hokkaido Sports Center**, 1999 (Architect: Kume Sekkei Co, Commissioning agency: Hokkaido Prefecture), Sapporo, Japan

39   **Sphere**, 1997 (Architect: Ellerbe Becket, Commissioning agency: The University of Minnesota), Carlson School of Business,
       University of Minnesota, 295 Humphrey Center, 271 19th Avenue South, Minneapolis, Minnesota, USA

41   **Broadway Pumphouse Sculpture**, 2000 (Commissioning agency: The City and County of Denver), Denver, Colorado, USA

BRAD GOLDBERG   42

43   **Continuum**, 2000 (Architect: Ellerbe Becket, Commissioning agency: Ryan Companies US and US Bancorp
       Piper Jaffray as part of the Minneapolis Beautiful Project), 800 Nicolett Street, Minneapolis, Minnesota, USA

45   **Bloomington Waters**, 1996 (Commissioning agency: the City of Bloomington for the Percentage for Art Program),
       New City Hall, Bloomington, Indiana, USA

46   **Prince of Peace Catholic Community**, 1994 (Architect: Cunningham Architects, Commissioning agency: the
       Prince of Peace Catholic Community), Prince of Peace Peace Catholic Community, Plano, Texas, USA

48   **Pegasus Plaza**, 1994 (Landscape architect: Luiz Sergio Santana, Commissioning agency: Dallas Institute of Humanities
       and Culture and the City of Dallas), City Center, Dallas, Texas, USA

47   **Mears Park**, 1993 (Commissioning agency: Department of Park and Recreation of the City of Saint Paul), Lowertown,
       St Paul, Minnesota, USA

Douglas Hollis 50

51   **A Sound Garden**, 1983 (Commissioning agency: National Oceanic Association and Atmospheric Administration),

       National Oceanic Association and Atmospheric Administration, Seattle, Washington, USA

52   **Water Songs**, 1996 (Architect: Stevens Williams, MBT Architects, Commissioning agency: General Services

       Administration Art in Architecture Program), US Geological Survey, Menlo Park, California, USA

53   **Oionos**, 1997, San Jose Repertory Theater, San Jose, California, USA

54   **Mountain Mirage**, 1999 (Technical Design by Chuck Schardt and Allan Wilson, Architect: Fentress Bradburn & Associates,

       Commissioning agency: DIA Public Art Program), Denver International Airport, Denver, Colorado, USA

56   **Tidal Park**, 1988 (With artist Charles Fahlen, Commissioning agency: City of Port Townsend), Port Townsend, Washington, USA

57   **Weather Pavilion**, 1993 (Commissioning agency: New York City School Construction Authority), PS/IS 2180, Roosevelt Island,

       New York, USA

Kristin Jones and Andrew Ginzel 58

59   **Metronome**, 1999 (Commissioning agency: The Related Companies with the participation of The Public Art Fund and the

       Municipal Art Society), Union Square South, 12th Street between Arch and Race Streets, Philadelphia, Pennsylvania, USA

60   **Oculus**, 1999 (Commissioning agency: The Arts for Transit Program of the Metropolitan Transportation Authority),

       World Trade Center, Park Place, Chambers Street Subway Station, New York, New York, USA

62   **Sounding**, 1994 (Architect: Daniel Brown, Commissioning agency: The Arts for Transit Program of the Metropolitan Transportation

       Authority), World Trade Center, Park Place, Chambers Street Subway Station, New York, New York, USA,

63   **Parenthesis**, 1998 (Commissioning agency: Midwest Express Center), Midwest Express Center, Milwaukee, Wisconsin, USA

65   **Mnemonics**, 1992 (Architect: Cooper Robertson & Partners, Commissioning agency: Battery Park City Authority,

       New City Board of Education, New York City Percentage for Art Program), Stuyvesant High School, New York, New York, USA

Stacy Levy 66

67   **Seeing the Path of the Wind**, 1991 (Commissioning agency: Richard Torchia, Curator, Moore College of Art and Design),

       Moore College of Art and Design, Philadelphia, Pennsylvania, USA

69   **Watercourse**, 1996 (Commissioning agency: Rosenwold Wolf Gallery), Rosenwold Wolf Gallery, University of the Arts,

       Philadelphia, Pennsylvania, USA

70   **What's in the Wind**, 1991 (Commissioning agency: The Springside School), The Springside School, Chestnut Hill,

       Philadelphia, Pennsylvania, USA

71   **Medal of Honor Memorial for Pennsylvania Recipients**, 1997 (Commissioning agency: Department of General Services

       for the Commonwealth of Pennsylvania, Capitol Complex, Harrisburg, Pennsylvania, USA

Winifred Lutz 72

73   **Correspondence/Congruence (Paradigm)**, 1995 (Commissioning agency: Cincinnati Contemporary Arts Center),

       Cincinnati Contemporary Arts Center, Cincinnati, Ohio, USA

74   **Site Unseen/Fluid Bodies**, 1998 (Commissioning agency: The College of DuPaige), Art Center of the College of DuPaige,

       DuPaige, Illinois, USA

75   **The Garden**, 1992–1997 (Commissioning agency: The Mattress Factory, with assistance from among others,

       The National Endowment for the Arts, and the Pew Fondation), The Mattress Factory, Pittsburgh, Pennsylvania, USA

76   **Reclamation Garden**, 1996 (Commissioning agency: Abington Art Center, with among others, the National Endowment

       for the Arts, and The Andy Warhol Foundation) Abington Art Center, Abington, Pennsylvania, USA

77   **Threshold/Interface/Transition, (When)** ,1997 (Commissioning agency: The Institute of Contemporary Art),

       Institute of Contemporay Art, University of Pennsylvania, Philadelphia, Pennsylvania, USA

WILLIAM MAXWELL — 78

79   **Echo**, 1999 (Commissioning agency: United States General Services Administration, Art in Architecture Program, Washington, DC), National Oceanic and Atmospheric Administration Facility, Boulder, Colorado, USA

80   **Endangered**, 1994 (Commissioning agency: University of West Florida), Center for Fine and Performing Arts, University of West Florida, Pensacola, Florida, USA

81   **Pandora**, 1989 (Architect: Bernard Maybeck), Capp Street Project and the Exploratorium, Palace of Fine Arts, San Francisco, California, USA

ANNA VALENTINA MURCH — 82

83   **Skydance**, 1995 (Architect: Fentress Bradburn & Associates, Commissioning agency: Denver International Airport Public Art Program, administered through the Major's Commission/Office of Art, Culture and Film for the City and County of Denver), Great Hall, Denver International Airport, Denver, Colorado, USA

85   **Cycles**, 1997 (Commissioning agency: Percent for Art Program of the New York City Department of cultural Affairs and the New York City Department of Design and Construction) Queens Civic Courthouse, Jamaica, Queens, New York, USA

87   **Skytones**, 1998 (Commissioning agency: The Seattle Arts Commission with added funding from Seattle Light), Third Avenue Arcade of Benaroya Hall, Seattle, Washington, USA

89   **Light Passageway**, 1993 (Landscape architect: Austin Tao Associates, Electrical engineer: Bob Banaskeck, Commissioning agency: Washington University Medical Center and Administered through Arts in Transit, Bi State Development Agency and Metlink), St Louis Rail Metro Rail, St Louis, Missouri, USA

90   **Memorial Union North Courtyard**, 1993 (With artist Douglas Hollis, Landscape Architect: Hargreaves Associates, Commissioning agency: University of California, Davis), University of California, Davis, California, USA

JODY PINTO — 92

93   **Boone Sculpture Garden**, 1995–2000 (Commissioning agency: Pasadena City College, Architects: Maris Peika and Morris I Sato), Pasadena City College, Pasadena, California, USA

94   **Beacon Overlook and Restrooms**, 1995–2001 (Landscape architect/Planners: Wallace, Roberts & Todd, Architect: Maris Peika and Architect: Morris/Sato Studio, Commissioning agency: City of Santa Monica and the Santa Monica Cultural Affairs Division), Santa Monica, California, USA

95   **Lantern Bridge**, 1995–2001 (Architect: Morris/Sato Studio, Commissioning agency: City of San Antonio) San Antonio Convention Center, San Antonio, Texas, USA

97   **Light Islands**, 1999 (Architect: Morris/Sato Studio, Commissioning agency: Art Front Gallery and City of Tokamachi), Echigo-Tsumari, Tokamachi City, Nigata Prefecture, Japan

ANTONETTE ROSATO — 98

99   **The Pattern that Connects**, 1995 (Commissioning agency: A.I.R. Gallery and C.U. Gallery, University of Colorado), A.I.R. Gallery, New York, New York, USA and C.U. Gallery, University of Colorado, Boulder, Colorado, USA

100   **Immigrant Desire/American Longing: The Vestibule**, 1998 (Video credit: William T. Gilbert, Commissioning agency: Metamedia Plasy), Plasy, Czech Republic

101   **Immigrant Desire/American Longing: The Return**, 1998 (A collaboration with artist William T. Gilbert, Commissioning agency: Metamedia Plasy), Plasy, Czech Republic

103   **Middle Knowledge**, 1999 (Commissioning agency: Museum of Contemporary Art, Denver) Museum of Contemporary Art, Denver, Denver, Colorado, USA

104   **Kinetic Light/Air Curtain**, 1994 (A collaboration of Antonette Rosato and William J. Maxwell, Architect: Fentress Bradburn & Associates, Commissioning agency: The Public Art Program of the City and County of Denver), Denver International Airport, Denver, Colorado, USA

Dean Ruck 106

107   **Big Bubble**, 1998 (Architects: Team HOU, and Ray & Hollington Architects, Commissioning agency: Central Houston Civic Improvements Inc.), Sesquicentennial Park, Houston, Texas, USA

108   **O House**, 1995 (With artists: Dan Havel and Kate Petley, Commissioning agency: The Cultural Arts Council of Houston/Harris County), Texas Accountants and Lawyers for the Arts, Houston, Texas, USA

109   **Tree House**, 2000 (Commissioning agency: Project Row Houses), Houston, Texas, USA

111   **Jewel**, 2000 (With artist Debbie McNulty, Commissioning agency: Connemara Conservancy), Allen, Texas, USA

Norie Sato 112

113   **Dallas Convention Center Expansion Project**, 1993, (In collaboration with artists: Phillip Lamb, William J. Maxwell, and Garrison Roots, Architects: LMN Architects, and JPJ Architects, Commissioning agency: City of Dallas, Art in Public Places), Dallas, Texas, USA

115   **Biochemistry Waltz**, 1998 (Architects: Flad & Associates, Commissioning agency: Wisconsin Arts Board), University of Wisconsin Biochemistry Building, Madison, Wisconsin, USA

116   **Brief Cases**, 1998 (With artists: Tad Savinar, and Bill Will, Architects: SERA Architects, Commissioning agency: Regional Arts and Cultural Council, Portland), Portland City Hall, Portland, Oregon, USA

119   **Gallivan Plaza Light Rail Station**, 2000 (Commissioning agency: Salt Lake City Arts Council and UTA), Salt Lake City, Utah, USA

117   **Courthouse Station**, 2000 (Commissioning agency: Salt Lake City Arts Council and UTA), Salt Lake City, Utah, USA

PUBLIC ART PROGRAMS

Broward County Cultural Affairs Council 122

(Director: Kerry Kennedy, Consultant: Tin Ly), Cultural Affairs division, 100 S. Andrews Avenue, Sixth Fl, Fort Lauderdale, Florida, USA

124   **Calypso**, 1998 (Artist: Tobey Archer, Commissioning agency: Broward County Cultural Affairs Division), Port Everglades, Terminal 2, Fort Lauderdale, Florida, USA

123   **Accordant Zones**, 1994 (Artist: Barbara Neijna and Ned Smyth, Architect: Michael Shiff & Associates) Broward County Judicial Complex, Fort Lauderdale, Florida, USA

126   **Everglades Tresspass**, 2000 (Artist: Carl Cheng), Broward County Southwest Regional Library, Pembrook Pines, Florida, USA

127   **Light Cylinders**, 1996–2001 (Artist: Jody Pinto, Project architect: Michael Morris/Sato Studio), Fort Lauderdale/Hollywood International Airport, Fort Lauderdale, Florida, USA

City of San Diego Commission for Art and Culture 128

(Executive Director: Victoria Hamilton), 1010 2nd Avenue, Suite 555, San Diego, California, USA

129   **Metro Biosolids Center**, 1998 (Artist: Richard Turner, Commissioning agency: City of San Diego Metropolitan Wastewater Department), Metro Biosolids Center, San Diego, California, USA

130   **The Alvarado Garden**, 1998 (Artists: Robert Millar, Commissioning agency: City of San Diego Water Department), The Alvaradro Water Treatment Plant Reservoirs at Lake Murray, San Diego, California, USA

133   **Great Balboa Park Landfill Exposition**, 1997 (Artist: Cindy Zimmerman, Commissioning agency: City of San Diego Environmental Services Department), East Mesa of Balboa Park, San Diego, California, USA

CULTURAL ARTS COUNCIL OF HOUSTON   134
(Director: Debbie McNulty), Civic Art and Design Department, 3201 Allen Parkway, Houston, Texas, USA

135   **Countree Music**, 1999 (Artist: Terry Allen), George A. Bush Intercontinental Airport, Terminal A, South Concourse,
       Houston, Texas, USA

136   **Seven Wonders**, 1998 (Artist Mel Chin, Commissioning agency: Central Houston Civic Improvement, Inc,
       Architects: Tom Hou, Ray & Hollington, Fabricators: Ambox, Inc., Fabricators, Ambox, Inc., Richey Enterprise,
       Sesquicentennial Park, Houston, Texas, USA

138   **Elevator Core**, 2000 (Artist: Rachel Hecker), George A. Bush Intercontinental Airport, Houston, Texas, USA

139   **Metro Bus Shelter**, 1999 (Artists: Rachel Hecker, Benito Huerta and Richard Turner), Metro Bus Station, Houston, Texas, USA

MTA METRO ART   142
(Director: Maya Emsden), Metropolitan Transportation Authority, One Gateway Plaza, Los Angeles, California, USA

145   **Vermont/Santa Monica Station**, 1999 (Artist: Robert Millar, Design engineer: Richard Brady & Associates,
       Landscape architect: David Kemp & Associates, Architect: Platt/Whitelaw & Associates, Commissioning agency:
       Los Angeles Metropolitan Transportation Authority), Metro Red Line, Los Angeles, California, USA

146   **People Coming/People Going**, 1996, (Artist: Richard Wyatt, Commissioning agency: Los Angeles Metropolitan
       Transportation Authority) Wilshire/Western Station, Metro Red Line, Los Angeles, California, USA

149   **Crenshaw Stories**, 1995 (Artist: Buzz Spector, Architect: Caltrans, Commissioning agency: Los Angeles Metropolitan
       Transportation Authority), Crenshaw /I-105 Metro Rail Station, Metro Green Line, Los Angeles, California, USA

143   **I Dreamed I Could Fly**, 1993 (Artist: Jonathan Borofsky, Commissioning agency: Los Angeles Metropolitan
       Transportation Authority), Civic Center Metro Rail Station, Metro Red Line, Los Angeles, California, USA

MIAMI-DADE ART IN PUBLIC PLACES   150
(Executive Director: Ivan A. Rodriguez, Coordinator: Lea Nickless Verrecchia, Coordinator of Education and Community Outreach),
111 NW First Street, Suite 610, Miami, Florida, USA

151   **A Walk on the Beach**, Phase I, 1995, Phase II, 1999 (Artist: Michele Oka Doner, Architect: Spillis Candela & Partners,
       Commissioning agency: Miami-Dade Art in Public Places), Miami International Airport, Terminal A, Miami, Florida, USA

153   **36th Street Wall**, 1996 (Artist: Martha Schwartz, Architects: Howard Needles Tammen & Bergendoff Architects,
       Commissioning agency: Miami-Dade Art in Public Places), Miami International Airport, Miami, Florida, USA

154   **Harmonic Runway**, 1995 (Artist: Christopher Janney, Architect: Spillis Candela & Partners, Commissioning agency:
       Miami-Dade Art in Public Places), Miami International Airport, Miami, Florida, USA

157   **Aqua/Botanica**, 1997 (Artists: Ed Carpenter, Mike McCulloch and John Rogers, Architects: Perez and Perez,
       Commissioning agency: Miami-Dade Art in Public Places) Concourse H, Miami International Airport, Miami, Florida, USA

PHOENIX ARTS COMMISSION   158
(Director: Vanessa Mallory), 200 West Washington Street, 10th Floor, Phoenix, Arizona, USA

159   **Papago Park/City Boundary**, 1992 (Artist: Jody Pinto, Landscape architect: Steve Martino, Commissioning agency:
       Parks, Recreation & Library Percentage for Art Funds), Papago Park at McDowell Road and Galvin Parkway, Phoenix, Arizona, USA

161   **An Open Book**, 1996 (Artists: Mayme Kratz, Debra L. Hopkins, Valerie Badala Homer, Commissioning agency:
       City of Phoenix Library CIP Bond Fund), Juniper Branch Library, Phoenix, Arizona, USA

162   **Paradise Lane Bridge**,1998 (Artist: Linnea Glatt with HDR Engineering, Commissioning agency: City of Phoenix Street
       Transportation CIP Percent for Art funds), Phoenix, Arizona, USA

162   **The Grasshopper Bridge**, 1997 (Artist: Ed Carpenter, Commissioning agencies: City of Phoenix Street Transportation
       Department, Storm Sewer Capitol Improvement Program, Percentage for the Arts), 7th Avenue Pedestrian Bridge at
       Cave Creek Wash, Phoenix, Arizona, USA

163   **Nisbet Road Pedestrian Bridge**, 1998 (Artist: Laurie Lundquist in partnership with HDR Engineering,
       Commissioning agencies: Arizona Department of Transportation, City of Phoenix Transportation Capitol Improvement Program,
       Percentage for the Arts), Nisbet Road, Phoenix, Arizona, USA

San Francisco Arts Commission   164

(Public Art Program Director: Jill Manton with Senior Public Art Project Manager Susan Pontius), Public Art Program, 25 Vann Ness Avenue, Suite 240, San Franciso, California, USA

165   **Functional and Fantasy Stair/Cyclone Fragment**, 1996 (Artist: Alice Aycock, Architect: Pei, Cobb, Freed & Partners
        and Simon Martin-Vegue Winkelstein Morris, Commissioning agency: San Francisco Arts Commission),
        Periodicals Reading Room, San Francisco Main Library, San Francisco, California, USA

166   **Constellation**, 1996 (Artist: Nayland Blake, Architect: Pei, Cobb, Freed & Partners and Simon Martin-Vegue
        Winkelstein Morris, Lighting: Architectural Design Lighting, Commissioning agency: San Francisco Arts Commission),
        Grand Staircase Atrium, San Francisco Main Library, San Francisco, California, USA

167   **Jury Assembly Room**, 1997-98 (Artist: Lewis Desoto, Architect: Ross Drulis Architecture, Commissioning agency:
        San Francisco Arts Commission), Jury Assembly Room of the Civic Center Courthouse, San Francisco, California, USA

167   **Civic Center Court House Entry Doors, Security Gates, and Door Handles**, 1997–1998 (Artist: Albert Paley,
        Commissioning agency; San Francisco Arts Commission), Civic Center Court House Entrance Lobby,
        400 McAllister Street at Polk, San Francisco, California, USA

168   **Untitled**, 1996 (Artists: Ann Hamilton and Ann Chamberlain, Architect: Pei, Cobb, Freed & Partners, and
        Simon Martin-Vegue Winkelstein Morris, Commissioning agency: San Francisco Arts Commission),
        Diagonal Wall on the Third, Fourth and Fifth Floors of the San Francisco Main Library, San Francisco, California, USA

San Jose Public Art Program   170

(Mary Rubin, Senior Project Manager), Office of Cultural Affairs, 4 North Second Street, Suite 450, San Jose, California, USA

171   **Origin**, 1999 (Artists: Brad Goldberg, Beliz Brother and Joseph McShane, Architects: Legoretta Arquitectos
        with Steinberg Group, Commissioning agency: San Jose Public Art Program for the San Jose Arts Commission),
        Tech Museum of Innovation, 201 S Market Street, San Jose, California, USA

173   **Untitled**, 1999 (Artists: Ann Chamberlain and Victor Mario Zaballa, Architect: Del Campo & Maru,
        Commissioning agency: San Jose Public Art Program for the San Jose Arts Commission), Mexican Heritage Plaza,
        1700 Alum Rock Avenue, San Jose, California, USA

176   **Jump Cuts**, 1996 (Artists: Elizabeth Diller and Ricardo Scofidio, with Paul Lewis, Architect: Kenneth Rodriguez & Partners,
        Commissioning agency: San Jose Public Art Program for the San Jose Arts Commssion), United Artists Cineplex,
        201 S Second Street, San Jose, California, USA

PHOTOGRAPHY CREDITS

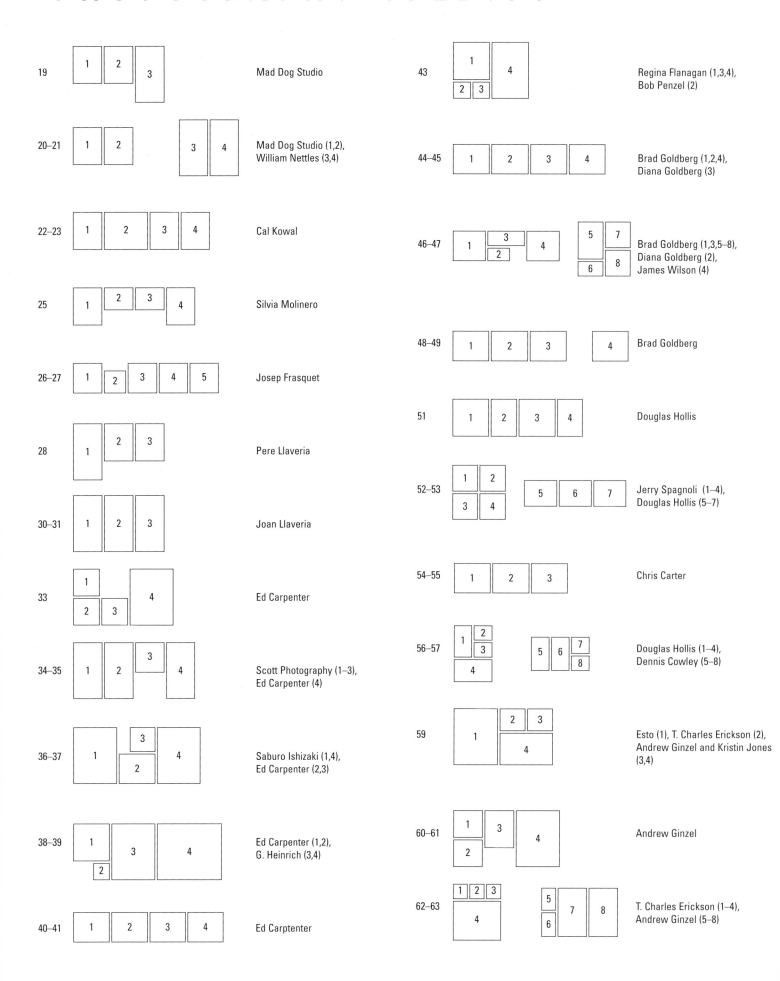

19 — Mad Dog Studio

20–21 — Mad Dog Studio (1,2), William Nettles (3,4)

22–23 — Cal Kowal

25 — Silvia Molinero

26–27 — Josep Frasquet

28 — Pere Llaveria

30–31 — Joan Llaveria

33 — Ed Carpenter

34–35 — Scott Photography (1–3), Ed Carpenter (4)

36–37 — Saburo Ishizaki (1,4), Ed Carpenter (2,3)

38–39 — Ed Carpenter (1,2), G. Heinrich (3,4)

40–41 — Ed Carptenter

43 — Regina Flanagan (1,3,4), Bob Penzel (2)

44–45 — Brad Goldberg (1,2,4), Diana Goldberg (3)

46–47 — Brad Goldberg (1,3,5–8), Diana Goldberg (2), James Wilson (4)

48–49 — Brad Goldberg

51 — Douglas Hollis

52–53 — Jerry Spagnoli (1–4), Douglas Hollis (5–7)

54–55 — Chris Carter

56–57 — Douglas Hollis (1–4), Dennis Cowley (5–8)

59 — Esto (1), T. Charles Erickson (2), Andrew Ginzel and Kristin Jones (3,4)

60–61 — Andrew Ginzel

62–63 — T. Charles Erickson (1–4), Andrew Ginzel (5–8)

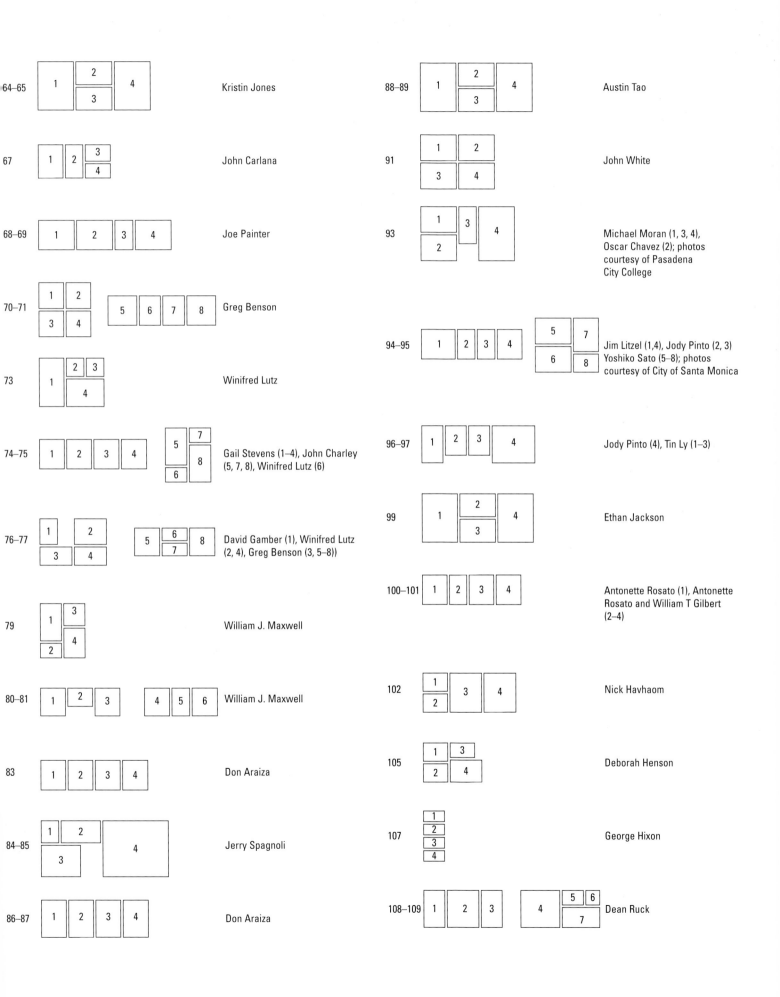

64–65 Kristin Jones

67 John Carlana

68–69 Joe Painter

70–71 Greg Benson

73 Winifred Lutz

74–75 Gail Stevens (1–4), John Charley (5, 7, 8), Winifred Lutz (6)

76–77 David Gamber (1), Winifred Lutz (2, 4), Greg Benson (3, 5–8))

79 William J. Maxwell

80–81 William J. Maxwell

83 Don Araiza

84–85 Jerry Spagnoli

86–87 Don Araiza

88–89 Austin Tao

91 John White

93 Michael Moran (1, 3, 4), Oscar Chavez (2); photos courtesy of Pasadena City College

94–95 Jim Litzel (1,4), Jody Pinto (2, 3) Yoshiko Sato (5–8); photos courtesy of City of Santa Monica

96–97 Jody Pinto (4), Tin Ly (1–3)

99 Ethan Jackson

100–101 Antonette Rosato (1), Antonette Rosato and William T Gilbert (2–4)

102 Nick Havhaom

105 Deborah Henson

107 George Hixon

108–109 Dean Ruck

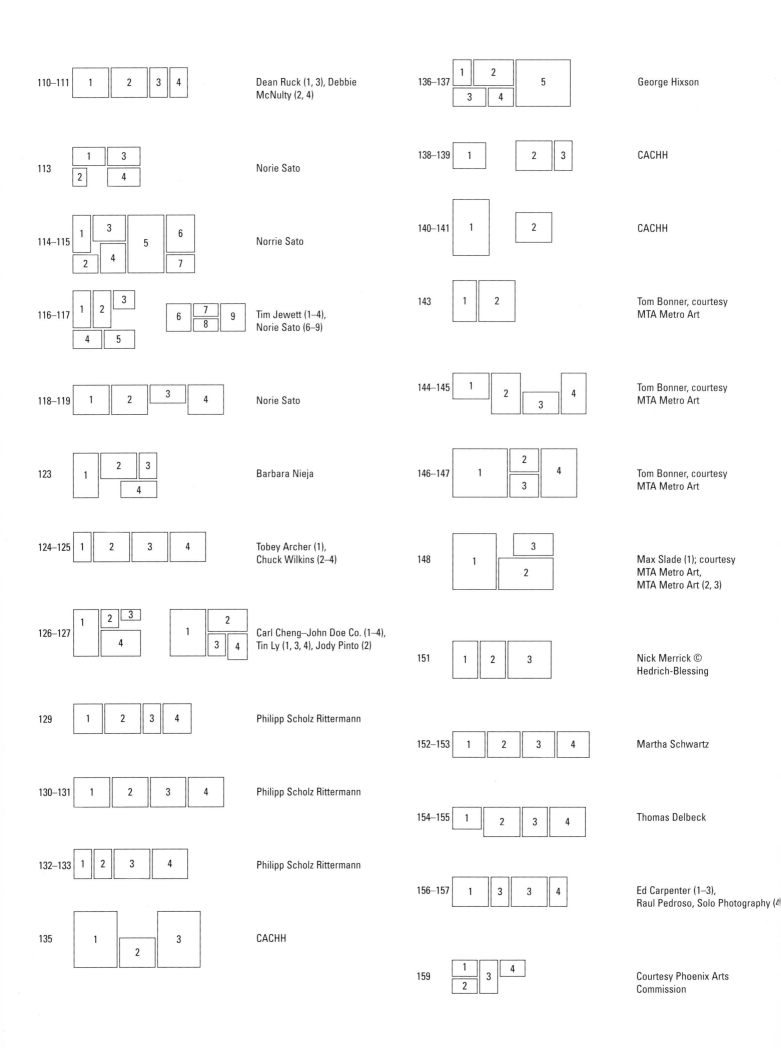

110–111 Dean Ruck (1, 3), Debbie McNulty (2, 4)

113 Norie Sato

114–115 Norrie Sato

116–117 Tim Jewett (1–4), Norie Sato (6–9)

118–119 Norie Sato

123 Barbara Nieja

124–125 Tobey Archer (1), Chuck Wilkins (2–4)

126–127 Carl Cheng–John Doe Co. (1–4), Tin Ly (1, 3, 4), Jody Pinto (2)

129 Philipp Scholz Rittermann

130–131 Philipp Scholz Rittermann

132–133 Philipp Scholz Rittermann

135 CACHH

136–137 George Hixson

138–139 CACHH

140–141 CACHH

143 Tom Bonner, courtesy MTA Metro Art

144–145 Tom Bonner, courtesy MTA Metro Art

146–147 Tom Bonner, courtesy MTA Metro Art

148 Max Slade (1); courtesy MTA Metro Art, MTA Metro Art (2, 3)

151 Nick Merrick © Hedrich-Blessing

152–153 Martha Schwartz

154–155 Thomas Delbeck

156–157 Ed Carpenter (1–3), Raul Pedroso, Solo Photography (4

159 Courtesy Phoenix Arts Commission

INDEX

160–161   [1] [2] [3] [4]   Fred Griffin

162   [1] [2] [3] [4] [5] [6] [7]   Craig Smith (1–4, 6,7), Dora Hernandez (5)

163   [1] [2] [3]   Craig Smith

165   [1] [2] [3] [4]   Craig Mole

166   [1] [2] [3] [4]   Craig Mole

167   [1] [2] [3] [4] [5] [6]   Lewis de Soto (1–3), Craig Mole (4–6)

168–169   [1] [2] [3] [4]   Craig Mole

171   [1] [2]   Lourdes Legoretta (1), Max Crumley (2)

172–173   [1] [2] [3] [4]   David Allen

174–175   [1] [2] [3]   David Allen

177   [1] [2] [3] [4]   Cesar Rubio

178–179   [1] [2] [3]   Cesar Rubio

Allen, Terry — **18**, 135
Arasa, Joan Llaveria I — **24**
Archer, Tobey — 124
Aycock, Alice — 165
Blake, Nayland — 166
Borofsky, Jonathan — 143
Brother, Beliz — 171
Carpenter, Ed — **32**, 157, 162
Chamberlain, Ann — 168, 173
Cheng, Carl — 126
Chin, Mel — 136
DeSoto, Lewis — 167
Diller, Elizabeth — 176
Fahlan, Charles — 56
Ginzel, Andrew — **58**
Glatt, Linnea — 162
Goldberg, Brad — **42**,171
Hamilton, Ann — 168
Hecker, Rachel — 138, 139
Hollis, Douglas — **50**
Homer, Valerie Vadala — 161
Hopkins, Debra L — 161
Huerta, Benito — 139
Janney, Chrstopher — 154
Jones/Ginzel — **58**
Jones, Kristin — **58**
Kratz, Mayme — 161
Levy, Stacy — **66**
Lewis, Paul — 176
Lundquist, Laurie — 163
Lutz, Winifred — **72**
McCulloch, Mike — 157
McShane, Joseph — 171
Maxwell, William (Bill) — **78**
Millar, Robert — 129, 145
Murch, Anna Valentina — **82**
Neijna, Barbara — 123
Oka Doner, Michele — 151
Paley, Albert — 167
Pinto, Jody — **92**, 127, 159
Rosato, Antonette — **98**
Ruck, Dean — **106**
Sato, Nori — **112**
Scofidio, Ricardo — 176
Smyth, Ned — 123
Spector, Buzz — 149
Schwartz, Martha — 153
Turner, Richard — 129, 139
Wyatt, Richard — 146
Zaballa, Victor Mario — 173
Zimmerman, Cindy — 133

Broward County Cultural Affairs Council — 122
City of San Diego Commission for Art and Culture — 128
Cultural Arts Council of Houston — 134
MTA Metro Art — 142
Miami-Dade Art in Public Places — 150
Phoenix Arts Commission — 158
San Francisco Arts Commission — 164
San Jose Public Art Program — 170

Bold numbers indicate artists featured in Artists section

A C K N O W L E D G M E N T S

IMAGES is pleased to present Designing the World's Best Public Art to its compendium of design and architectural publications. We wish to thank each participating artist and public art program for their invaluable contribution to this publication. ● Professor Roots notes the very generous contribution made by Jennifer Harding as assistant editor in the preparation of submissions for this book. ● Garrison Roots has a website: www.garrisonroots.com. Please visit this site to contact Garrison or obtain further information about the artists or programs featured in this book.